Dictionary of African Names

Vol.1

Meanings, Pronunciations and Origin

by
'Bunmi Adebayo

authorHOUSE™

1663 Liberty Drive, Suite 200
Bloomington, Indiana 47403
(800) 839-8640
www.AuthorHouse.com

First published by AuthorHouse 07/06/05

ISBN: 1-4208-4794-5 (sc)

Library of Congress Control Number: 2005905933

Printed in the United States of America
Bloomington, Indiana

This book is printed on acid-free paper.

FOREWORD

The quest for African distinct identity and need for integration among Africans on one hand and between Africans in diasporas and homelands on the other hand have been an ongoing issue. I am glad to be part of this solution to resolve the question. As a student and resident in the United states in the 70/80's, and currently a director/adjunct Professor in one of the colleges in Newark New Jersey, the melting pot of African, and African-American Culture, I am glad to witness the publication of this book that will further smoothen a growing interest in the origin and culture of Africans.

The rave of connection to the African continent by African-Americans dated back to 1859, when Mr. Martin. R. Delany's team visited West Africa and signed a treaty in Abeokuta Nigeria, to resettle African-Americans and thereby begin a mass exodus back to African homelands. This was recorded in the "Official Report of The Niger Valley Exploring Party", Chatham, Canada West, July 30, 1861,and published in New York by Thomas Hamilton. The connection continued till the era of Marcus Garver, W.B Dubois, and Malcolm X until the time of "Dashiki" top and Afro hairstyle which became symbols of connection to African heritage among African-Americans. The most interesting, and meaningful connection is the adoption of African names. One of the notable African American personalities that has African name is Mr. Kwame Nfume, former President of the NAACP. We can go on and mention thousands of efforts by Africans in Diasporas to identify with their African root. However, if we visit villages in Africa and inquire about the location of Africans taken away during slavery and middle passage, one will be stunned for lack of credible answer. Many could not account for the location of current descendants of those affected, not to talk of acknowledging the fact that America inhabits more than 30 Million Africans and Brazil, Haiti, Grenada, Trinidad and Tobago, Cuba have other African descendants in millions as well.

The onus lies in our hands as Africans to extend and strengthen these hands of fellowship and goodwill, by sharing our culture with our brothers and sisters in Diasporas. Most African students and visitors to America and Europe expose their names to the western world and other Africans as well. A lot of us have encountered (and we still do) mispronunciation and misspelling of our names.

What we face now is the distortion of African words, names and phrases and attendant extinction of their meanings and pronunciations. An example is "Sango" – God of iron, spelt "Xango" by the people of Yoruba descent in Brazil.

In a concerted effort by some of our dynamic leaders such as the President of Nigeria, Chief Olusegun Obasanjo, the President of Ghana, Chief John Kufuor, African leaders are now more than ever before focused on the continent. This is evidenced by the re-invigoration of the African Union (AU), formerly AOU. It is painful that most Africans of different cultures and nationalities encounter each other better in the Americas and Europe, rather than in Africa. To abate this, some African countries like Nigeria now have Ministries for African Integration and Co-Operatives to help with Integration.

This book "Dictionary of African Names Vol. 1" will be a reference for Africans African-American to understand each other, and at the same time serve as a tool for other cultures to understand Africans better. I will therefore recommend this book to everyone concerned about the African race and her very rich cultures.

Otunba Olusoga Onafowora
Director of Financial Operations,
Essex County College, Newark New Jersey.
Commissioner and Vice Chairman, Carteret Redevelopment Agency,
Carteret, Middlesex County, New Jersey

DEDICATION

This reference book is dedicated to all Africans both in the homelands and diasporas who wish we all know each other better, and my parents Chief, and Chief (Mrs) Adisa, and Oluseun Adebayo by allowing God to use them to bring me to life.

ACKNOWLEDGEMENT

I like to acknowledge all those Africans and people of African descent that shared their knowledge of names and meanings with me. I am particularly indebted to those that willingly offered to submit their names, meanings and pronunciations to my website: http://members.fortunecity.com/ bunmi_adebayo. If I decide to mention names, it will be a whole book again.

My gratitude also goes to my immediate family, 'Remi (my wife), 'Temilade, Oyinade, and Omolade, who shared some of tedious the moments during the compilation of the book. I wish to apologize to "Omo"(my baby), for my divided attention those times.

Thank you all.

'Bunmi Adebayo
Author

TABLE OF CONTENTS

ABOUT THE AUTHOR

Bunmi Adebayo a.k.a "OPJ" or "Opeji", a Nigerian-American is an alumnus of both the University of Ife, (Now OAU) Ile- Ife Nigeria, and University of Missouri- Columbia, Graduate School, in the United states where he graduated in International relations and New Media respectively. He's also taken Project management courses at the Rutgers University- New Brunswick NJ, also in the United States. 'Bunmi attended the prestigious Abeokuta Grammar School and Ogun State Polytechnic both in Abeokuta Nigeria, in the mid 70's and early 80's for his High school and "A" levels education respectively.

Bunmi, currently based in New Jersey in the United States was born in his native home town of Abeokuta, Ogun state Nigeria in the mid 60,s to a family of seven in which he is the second child. The author is married to his friend, 'Remi, (nee Macjob) and currently blessed with three children Temilade, Oyinade, and Omolade.

Bunmi has been working in Information technology as Web Administrator since the late 90,s with a stint at the Journal of Commerce (then, a subsidiary of London Economist) and XO communications, both in the United States.

His challenges in his days at the University of Ife on race and International relations culminated in his study of the history of the Africans in diasporas, especially North, South and Central America and the attendant effect on their country's international relations with Africa. This publication "Dictionary of African names Vol. I" is his contribution to the closure of the divide created by the middle passage and an eventual culturally connected committee of African nations both in the homeland and diasporas.

'Bunmi adores Chief Obafemi Awolowo (Late Nigerian Nationalist), and especially his popular saying 'After darkness comes glorious dawn".

'Bunmi Adebayo can be reached at opeji@hotmail.com.

INTRODUCTION

This book publishes thousands of African names, their ethnic groups, countries of origin, and their English phonetic pronunciations. The book is for those interested in African names and general readers seeking more knowledge about African culture or willing to recapture African heritage through name. It is a thorough exposure of African names and meanings. It encourages and stimulates people of both African and non-African descent into feeling comfortable about taking on such names.

The African naming tradition is a complex area that has been in focus in recent times, not as a need to resolve controversy but to correct the distortions and misnomer in its body of knowledge. Distortions in African names can be traced to the Middle passages, and the attendant forced assimilation of Africans to "Newfoundland". Moreover, the era of colonialism in the African continent did not help in articulating the meanings and origins of African names in the continent itself. A lot happened to even some Africans in the homeland in their inability to translate or appreciate their native names with the influx of missionaries to the continent of Africa, and a model of inferiority complex emanated whereby people were dropping their African names for the new baptismal names adopted in the new Christian religions. The other problems emanated from the Non-appreciation of African Names by new generation of Africans in Diaspora. The flow is for current generation of Africans in Diasporas to adopt or accept European or American names or western modified version ("Wally" for "Wole" or "Alan" for "Alani") of their names at work places.

There have been many attempts to re-write and rearticulate the African traditions to other parts of the world, of which naming system is just one of them. I often tell my friends and aquittances that the best ambassadors of a nation or culture is the people and not the offices of the High commissioners or ambassadors. The people of other cultures on the street are the real mirror of their nation or culture. One of the ways to get other cultures to appreciate you and your attendant origin is your ability to educate about who you are, where you come from and of course your culture. This instinct is one of the attendant reasons for this book. I used a lot of resources in the editing this book, among which are personal and phone interviews, oral tradition and many who have submitted their names to my website, http://members.fortunecity.com/bunmi_adebayo and, also helped to verify this. I will forever be grateful for their input. Other reason that informed me to put this together is the inadequacy is some other African Names books that probably lumped modified Afro-European names with authentic African names. Some of the books also were either region- centric, by mentioning names prevalent in some African regions to the detriment of others. My book touches on all the parts of the continent. In as much as African names and cultures are exhaustive and so diverse, I have endeavored to touch on all parts of the continent. This will be first volume, because it only contains a little over 2600 names. I hope to develop on this in volume two of the book. It will still be extremely difficult to find any source that collects and defines the meanings of over a million African names in English or any other western language. This attempt is one of many to document Africa, by Africans. Africa is a continent with thousands of cultures, traditions and languages. Names are reflection of the enriched African tradition. Unlike other parts of the world, virtually every African indigenous name has a distinct meaning or connotation.

There is popular adage among the Yoruba of Modern Nigeria that "the naming of a child is a reflection of family history or events". Therefore African names relate to personal and family relationships, new blessings, ceremonies, prayers, proverbs, number and sequence of offspring, physical and physiological nature of the newborn, mode of birth, gods and spirits, war, neighborhood relationships, bravery, magic, trees and wildlife, clan affiliation, as well as tragedies.

In modern African-American history, we have witnessed change of names to that of African. The first African-American to change his name in recorded United States history is a wealthy nineteenth century Boston shipbuilder who discarded his slave name, Slocum, in favor of his father's name, Kofi: A Ghanaian (Akan, Ewe) name which means, a male born on Friday. The trend has been common since then. It is noteworthy to mention Chokwe Lumumba, Sundiata Acoli, Madhubuti Kwame Ture, Oba T'Shaka, Dr. Imari Abubakar Obadele, Dr. Kobi Kazembe, Fasina Falade. There is also the late Royal Highness, Oba Efuntola Oseijeman Adelabu Adefunmi who passed away on Thursday, February 10, 2005 at Oyotunji African Village in Beaufort County, South Carolina. The civil rights leader Rev. Ralph David Abernathy, who happens to be Dr. Martin Luther King, Jr.'s best friend and his successor as head of the Southern Christian Leadership Conference named his youngest child Kwame Luthuli. In the African homeland, there is the late billionaire dictator, who at age 42 cast off the name of his Belgian name, Joseph-Desire, in favor of Mobutu

Sese Seko. We can see a trend that has been on going and this book has come to aid. I am actually confident that Africans in diasporas and those at home will be more comfortable picking their African names.

I once defined the "The essence of life, to be problem solving " and subsequent generations will evaluate our effort in resolving the daily occurring problems. Therefore this attempt is my effort to "resolve a problem", which is the essence of life.

'Bunmi Adebayo
Author

AFRICAN FEMALE NAMES

BOTSWANA

Name	Pronunciation	Meaning	Origin	Region
Dikeledi	Dee-KEH-leh-dee	Tears	Tswana	South Africa
Goitsemedime.	Khoat-say-moh-DEE-meh	God knows	Tswana	South Africa
Kagiso	Kah-GHEE-soh	Peace	Tswana	South Africa
Kefilwe	Kay-FEEL-weh	I am given	Tswana	South Africa
Lerato	Leh-RAH-toh	Love	Tswana	South Africa
Montsho	MOAN-shoh	Black	Tswana	South Africa
Moswen	MOHSS-when	White	Tswana	South Africa
Mpho	M-POH	Gift	Tswana	South Africa
Tale	TAH-leh	Green	Tswana	South Africa

ETHIOPIA

Name	Pronunciation	Meaning	Origin
Amira	Ah-meer-rah	Princess	Arabic
Yenee	Yah - nay	Mine	Ethiopain
Tenagne	Ta-non-ya	Gold	Amharic
Ayana	Ayana	Beautiful flower	Ethiopian
Aisha	Ahe-sha	Life	Arabic or Swahili

GHANA

Name	Pronunciation	Meaning	Origin	Region
Aba	Ah-BAH	Born on Thursday	Fante	West Africa
Ababuo	Ah-bah-BOO-oh	Child that keeps coming back	Ewe	West Africa

3

GHANA

Name	Pronunciation	Meaning	Origin	Region
Abam	Ah-BAHM	Second child after twins	Twi	West Africa
Abena	Ah-beeh-NAH	Born on Tuesday	Akan	West Africa
Adowa	Ah-doh-WAH	Born on a Tuesday	Akan	West Africa
Adwoa	Ah-dwoh-AH	Born on a Monday	Fante	West Africa
Afafa	Ah-FAH-fah	First child of second husband	Ewe	West Africa
Afia	Ah-FEE-ah	Born on Friday	Ewe	West Africa
Afryea	Ah-FRY-yah	Born during good times	Ewe	West Africa
Afua	Ah-FOO-ah	Born on Friday	Ewe	West Africa
Akosua	Ah-KOH-soo-ah	Born on Sunday	Ewe	West Africa
Akua	Ah-KOO-ah	Born on Wednesday	Ewe	West Africa
Akwete	Ah-KWEH-the	Elder of twins	Ga	West Africa
Akwokwo	Ah-KWO-kwoh	Younger of twins	Ga	West Africa
Ama	AH-mah	Born on Saturday	Ewe	West Africa
Antobam	Ahn-toh-BAHM	Posthumous child	Fante	West Africa
Baba	BAH-bah	Born on Thursday	Fante	West Africa
Boahinmaa	Bwa-HIN-mah	One who has left her community	Ewe	West Africa
Do	Doh	First child after twins	Ewe	West Africa
Dofi	DOH-fee	Second child after twins	Ewe	West Africa
Efia	Eh-FEE-ah	Born on Friday	Fante	West Africa
Enyonyam	EN-yo-nam	It is good for me	Ewe	West Africa
Esi	Eh-SEE	Born on Sunday	Fante	West Africa
Falala	Fah-LAH-la	Born into abundance	Fulani	West Africa
Kakra	Kah-KRAH	Younger of twins	Fante	West Africa

GHANA

Name	Pronunciation	Meaning	Origin	Region
Kukua	Koo-KOO-ah	Born on Wednesday	Fante	West Africa
Kunto	KOON-toh	Third child	Twi	West Africa
Lumusi	Loo-moo-SEE	Born face downwards	Ewe	West Africa
Mama	Mah-AMH	Born on Saturday	Fante	West Africa
Mawusi	Mah-woo-SEE	In the hands of God	Ewe	West Africa
Morowa	Moh-ROH-wah	Queen	Akan	West Africa
Nanyanika	Nah-YAHM-kah	God's gift	Ewe	West Africa
Nyankomago	Ng-yank-oh-MAH-goh	Second child after twins	Twi	West Africa
Ozigbodi	Oh-ZEE-gboh-dee	Patience	Ewe	West Africa
Panyin	Pahn-YEEN	Elder of twins	Fante	West Africa
Sorwa	Sair-WAH	Noble woman	Ewe	West Africa
Sisi	See-SEE	Born on a Sunday	Fante	West Africa
Tawiah	TAH-wee-ah	First child after twins	Ga	West Africa
Thema	TEH-mah	Queen	Akan	West Africa
Yaa	YAH-ah	Born on Thursday	Ewe	West Africa
Ye	YEH-eh	Elder of twins	Ewe	West Africa

COTE D'IVOIRE

Name	Pronunciation	Meaning	Origin	Region
Kali	KAH-lee	Energetic	Senufo	West Africa

KENYA

Name	Pronunciation	Meaning	Origin	Region
Abuya	AH-boo-yah	Born when the garden was overgrown	Luo	East Africa
Achieng	AH-chee-eng	Born at mid day	Luo	East Africa
Adongo	AH-dohn-goh	Second of twins	Luo	East Africa
Akello	AH-keh-loh	Born after twins	Luo	East Africa
Akeyo	AH-keh-yoh	Born during the harvest	Luo	East Africa
Akinyi	AH-key-nyee	Born in the early morning	Luo	East Africa
Akoth	AH-koh-th	Born during the rainy season	Luo	East Africa
Aluna	Ah-LOO-nah	Come here	Mwera	East Africa
Aluoch	AH-loo-oh ch	Born on a overcast morning	Luo	East Africa
Amondi	AH-mohn-dee	Born at dawn	Luo	East Africa
Angweng	AHNG-when	Born during the time of white ants	Luo	East Africa
Anindo	AH-neen-doh	Mother slept alot during pregnancy	Luo	East Africa
Anyango	AHN-yahn-go	Born about mid day	Luo	East Africa
Apiyo	AH-pee-oh	First of twins	Luo	East Africa
Arogo	AH-roh-goh	Mother nagged alot during pregnancy	Luo	East Africa
Athiambo	AH-thee-ahm-boh	Born late in the evening	Luo	East Africa
Atieno	AH-tee-eh-no	Born at night	Luo	East Africa
Awino	AH-wee-noh	Born with the cord around them	Luo	East Africa

KENYA

Name	Pronunciation	Meaning	Origin	Region
Awiti	AH-wee-tee	Born after misfortune	Luo	East Africa
Awour	AH-woh-rr	Born in the mid morning	Luo	East Africa
Barongo	BAH-rohn-goh	Younger of twin	Kisii	East Africa
Gathoni	GAH-tho-nee	She is an in law	Kikuyu	East Africa
Jata	JAH-tah	Star	Kikuyu	East Africa
Jumapili	Joo-mah-PEE-lee	Born on Sunday	Mwera	East Africa
Kainda	Kah-EEN-dah	Hunter's daughter		East Africa
Kanika	Kah-NEE-kah	Black cloth	Mwera	East Africa
Kaweria	Kah-WEH-ree-ah	Loving one	Meru	East Africa
Kerubo	KEH-roo-boh	Born on the plain	Kisii	East Africa
Kioni	KEO-nee	She who see	Kikuyu	East Africa
Kwamboka	KWAHM-boh-kah	Born while crossing a river	Kisii	East Africa
Makena	Mah-KEH-nah	Happy one	Kikuyu	East Africa
Mong'ina	MOHN-ngee-nah	My mother	Kisii	East Africa
Moraa	MOH-rah	Fun loving	Kisii	East Africa
Mugure	MOH-goh-reh	Already purchased	Meru	East Africa
Mukami	MOH-kah-mee	A milk maid	Kikuyu	East Africa
Mukondi	Moh-KOH-dee	A dancer	Kikuyu	East Africa
Mumbi	MOH-bee	Creator, mother of the people	Kikuyu	East Africa
Murigo	MOH-ree-goh	This is a load	Kikuyu	East Africa
Murugi	MOH-roo-gee	She cooks	Kikuyu	East Africa
Muthoni	MOH-tho-nee	She is an in law	Kikuyu	East Africa
Nafula	Nah-foo-LAH	Born during the rainy season		East Africa
Ngendo	Nng-eh-DOH	A traveller	Kikuyu	East Africa

KENYA

Name	Pronunciation	Meaning	Origin	Region
Ngina	GHEH-nah	One who serves	Kikuyu	East Africa
Njeri	JEH-ree	Daughter of a warrior	Kikuyu	East Africa
Njoki	JOH-key	She who returned	Kikuyu	East Africa
Nyaguthii	NYAH-goh-thee-ay	A traveler	Kikuyu	East Africa
Nyakio	NYAH-kay-oh	Hard working	Kikuyu	East Africa
Nyambura	NYAH-boo-rah	Born of the rain	Kikuyu	East Africa
Nyanjera	NYAHN-jeh-rah	Born on the way	Kisii	East Africa
Nyathera	NYAH-the-rah	She survived	Kisii	East Africa
Nyawira	NYAH-way-rah	Hard worker	Kikuyu	East Africa
Nyokabi	NYOH-kah-bee	Of the Maasai people	Kikuyu	East Africa
Waceera	WAH-sheh-rah	Wanderer	Kikuyu	East Africa
Wairimu	WAH-ee-ree-moh	One of the nine founders of the Agikuyu people	Kikuyu	East Africa
Waitherero	WAH-ee-theh-reh-roh	From the rivers flow	Kikuyu	East Africa
Wakiuru	WAH-kay-oh-roh	One of the nine founders of the Agikuyu people	Kikuyu	East Africa
Wambui	Wah-MBOH-ee	Singer of songs	Kikuyu	East Africa
Wamuhu	WAH-moh-hoo	Born of ashes	Kikuyu	East Africa
Wamuiru	WAH-moh-ee-roh	Dark skinned beauty	Kikuyu	East Africa
Wamweru	WAHM-weh-roh	Light skinned	Kikuyu	East Africa
Wangai	WAH-gah-ee	Born of God	Kikuyu	East Africa
Wangari	WAH-gah-ray	A leopard	Kikuyu	East Africa
Wangera	WAH-jay-rah	A traveler	Kikuyu	East Africa
Wangu	WAHN-goh	She gathers the firewood	Kikuyu	East Africa

KENYA

Name	Pronunciation	Meaning	Origin	Region
Wanja	WAH-jah	The one from without	Kikuyu	East Africa
Wanjeri	WAH-jeh-ree	Born of Njeri	Kikuyu	East Africa
Wanjiku	WAHN-gee-koh	One of the nine founders of the Agikuyu people	Kikuyu	East Africa
Wanjiru	WAHN-gee-roh	One of the nine founders of the Agikuyu people	Kikuyu	East Africa
Wokabi	WOH-kah-bee	She is of the Maasai	Kikuyu	East Africa

KENYA TANZANIA

Name	Pronunciation	Meaning	Origin	Region
Abla	AH-blah	A wild rose	Swahili	East Africa
Adhra	AH-drah	Apology	Swahili	East Africa
Adila	AH-dee-lah	Just, upright	Swahili	East Africa
Adimu	AH-DEE-moo	Rare	Swahili	East Africa
Adin	Ah-DEEN	Decorative	Swahili	East Africa
Adla	AHD-lah	Justice	Swahili	East Africa
Afaafa	AH-fah-fah	Virtue	Swahili	East Africa
Afifa	AH-fee-fah	Virtuous, pure	Swahili	East Africa
Afiya	Ah-FEE-yah	Health	Swahili	East Africa
Afrika	AH-free-kah	Africa	Swahili	East Africa
Afua	AH-foo-ah	Forgiveness	Swahili	East Africa
Afya	AHF-yah	Health	Swahili	East Africa
Ahadi	Ah-HAH-dee	With much promise	Swahili	East Africa
Aida	AH-ee-dah	Gain, advantage	Swahili	East Africa
Ainra	AH-een-rah	Lasting power	Swahili	East Africa
Aisha	Ah-EE-shah	She is life	Swahili	East Africa

KENYA TANZANIA

Name	Pronunciation	Meaning	Origin	Region
Ajia	Ah-jee-AH	Quick, fast	Swahili	East Africa
Akilah	AH-kee-lah	Intelligent, one who reasons	Swahili	East Africa
Akili	Ah-KEE-lee	Intelligent	Swahili	East Africa
Aliya	Ah-lee-AH	Exalted	Swahili	East Africa
Almasi	Al-MAH-see	Diamond	Swahili	East Africa
Amali	AH-mah-lee	Hope	Swahili	East Africa
Amana	AH-mah-nah	Trust	Swahili	East Africa
Amaziah	Ah-MAH-zee-ah	Extraordinary	Swahili	East Africa
Amina	Ah-mee-NAH	Trustworthy, faithful	Swahili	East Africa
Aminah	Ah-MEE-nah	She is trustworthy	Swahili	East Africa
Aminali	Ah-MEE-nah	Honest, faithful	Swahili	East Africa
Aminifu	AH-mee-nee-FUH	Faithful	Swahili	East Africa
Amira	Ah-mee-RAH	Princess	Swahili	East Africa
Amne	AHM-neh	Secure	Swahili	East Africa
Aneesa	Ah-nee-SAH	Companion	Swahili	East Africa
Angavu	Ahn-GAH-voo	Shining one	Swahili	East Africa
Anisa	Ah-nee-SAH	Friendly	Swahili	East Africa
Anisun	Ah-NEE-sun	Friendly	Swahili	East Africa
Arafa	AH-rah-fah	Knowledgeable	Swahili	East Africa
Arifa	AH-ree-fah	Knowledgeable	Swahili	East Africa
Arusi	Ah-ROO-see	Born at the time of a wedding	Swahili	East Africa
Asali	Ah-SAH-li	Sweet honey	Swahili	East Africa
Asatira	Ah-SAH-tee-rah	Legend, saga	Swahili	East Africa
Asha	AH-shah	Life	Swahili	East Africa
Ashura	Ah-SHOO-rah	Companion	Swahili	East Africa
Asilia	Ah-see-LEE-ah	Honest	Swahili	East Africa
Asiya	AH-see-yah	Console	Swahili	East Africa
Asma	AH-smah	Higher, more exalted	Swahili	East Africa

KENYA TANZANIA

Name	Pronunciation	Meaning	Origin	Region
Asmahani	AHSS-mah-ha-nee	Exalted	Swahili	East Africa
Asumini	Ah-soo-MEE-nee	Jasmine	Swahili	East Africa
Asya	AHSS-yah	Born at a time of grief	Swahili	East Africa
Atiya	AH-tee-yah	Gift	Swahili	East Africa
Awena	AH-weh-nah	Gentle	Swahili	East Africa
Aza	AH-zah	Powerful	Swahili	East Africa
Aziza	Ah-ZEE-zah	Precious	Swahili	East Africa
Badriya	BAH-dree-yah	Moorlike	Swahili	East Africa
Bahati	Bah-HAH-tee	My luck is good	Swahili	East Africa
Bahiya	BAH-hee-yah	Beautiful	Swahili	East Africa
Barke	BAH-keh	Blessings	Swahili	East Africa
Basha	BAH-shah	Act of God	Swahili	East Africa
Bashaam	Bah-SHAM	Rich	Swahili	East Africa
Bashira	BAH-shee-RAH	Predictor of good news	Swahili	East Africa
Basma	BAHS-mah	A smile	Swahili	East Africa
Batuuli	BAH-tool-ee	Maiden	Swahili	East Africa
Baya	BAH-yah	Ugly	Swahili	East Africa
Bayyina	BAY-ee-nah	Evidence, proof	Swahili	East Africa
Bebi	BEH-bee	Baby	Swahili	East Africa
Bia	BEE-ah	Home, environment	Swahili	East Africa
Bimbaya	BEEM-bah-yah	Ugly lady	Swahili	East Africa
Bimdogo	BEEM-doh-goh	Young lady	Swahili	East Africa
Bimkubwa	Beem-KOOB-wah	Great lady	Swahili	East Africa
Bimnono	BEEM-no-no	Fat lady	Swahili	East Africa
Bishara	BEE-shah-rah	Good news	Swahili	East Africa
Bitisururu	BEE-tee-soo-roo-roo	Daughter of happiness	Swahili	East Africa
Bititi	BEE-tee-tee	Strqng lady	Swahili	East Africa

KENYA TANZANIA

Name	Pronunciation	Meaning	Origin	Region
Biubwa.	BEE-ooh-bwah	Baby-like, soft and smooth	Swahili	East Africa
Buqisi	BOOH-kee-see	Queen of Sabaa	Swahili	East Africa
Busara	BUH-sah-rah	Wisdom	Swahili	East Africa
Bushira	BOO-shee-rah	Announcer of good news	Swahili	East Africa
Chaniya	CHAH-nee-yah	Rich	Swahili	East Africa
Chausiku	Chah-oo-SEE-koo	Born at night	Swahili	East Africa
Chausiku	Chah-oo-SEE-koo	Born at night	Swahili	East Africa
Chiku	CHEE-koo	Chatterer	Swahili	East Africa
Chuki	CHOO-kee	Born when there was animosity	Swahili	East Africa
Dabiku	DAH-bee-koo	Sacrifice, offering	Swahili	East Africa
Dafina	DAH-fee-nah	Valuable, precious	Swahili	East Africa
Dalali	DAH-lah-lee	Broker	Swahili	East Africa
Dalila	Dah-LEE-lah	Gentleness is her soul	Swahili	East Africa
Dalili	Dah-LEE-lee	Sign, omen	Swahili	East Africa
Damisi	DAH-mee-see	Sociable, cheerful	Swahili	East Africa
Dawa	Dah-WAH	Medleine	Swahili	East Africa
Dhakiya	THA-kee-yah	Intelligent	Swahili	East Africa
Dhambizao	THAM-bee-zah-oh	The sins are their's	Swahili	East Africa
Dhuriya	THU-ree-yah	Descendant	Swahili	East Africa
Dodo	DOH-doh	Lovable, large and round	Swahili	East Africa
Doli	DOH-lee	Doll	Swahili	East Africa
Ducha	DOO-chah	Little	Swahili	East Africa
Duni	DOO-nee	Small	Swahili	East Africa
Durah	Doo-RAH	Pearl	Swahili	East Africa
Durra	Doo-RAH	Large pearl	Swahili	East Africa

KENYA TANZANIA

Name	Pronunciation	Meaning	Origin	Region
Eidi	EH-ee-dee	Festival, festivity	Swahili	East Africa
Eshe	EH-sheh	Life	Swahili	East Africa
Etana	Eh-TAH-nah	Strong one	Swahili	East Africa
Fadhila	FAH-dee-lah	Outstanding, abundance	Swahili	East Africa
Fadhili	FAH-dee-lee	Kindness, goodwill	Swahili	East Africa
Fadiya	FAH-dee-yah	Redeemer	Swahili	East Africa
Fahari	Fah-HAH-ree	Splendour	Swahili	East Africa
Fahima	Fah-HEEM-ah	Learned, understands	Swahili	East Africa
Faida	FAH-ee-dah	Benefit	Swahili	East Africa
Faika	FAH-ee-kah	Superior	Swahili	East Africa
Faiza.	FAH-ee-zah	Victorious	Swahili	East Africa
Faizah	FAH-ee-zah	Victorious	Swahili	East Africa
Fakhta	FAHK-tah	Pierce	Swahili	East Africa
Fanaka	Fah-nah-KAH	Prosperity	Swahili	East Africa
Fanikia	Fah-NEE-kee-ah	Prosperity	Swahili	East Africa
Faraja	FAH-rah-jah	Relief	Swahili	East Africa
Farashuu	FAH-rah-shoo	Butterfly	Swahili	East Africa
Farida	FAH-ree-dah	Unique	Swahili	East Africa
Farisi	FAH-ree-see	Competent, capable	Swahili	East Africa
Fasaha	Fah-SAH-hah	Eloquence	Swahili	East Africa
Fathiya	Fah-THEE-yah	Triumph	Swahili	East Africa
Fatima	FAH-tee-mah	Daughter of the Prophet Mohammed	Swahili	East Africa
Fatuma	Fah-TOO-mah	Daughter of the Prophet Mohammed	Swahili	East Africa
Fauziya	FAH-ooh-zee-yah	Successful	Swahili	East Africa
Feruzi	Feh-ROO-zee	Turquoise	Swahili	East Africa
Fidela	FEE-deh-lah	Feminine of Fidel, faithful	Swahili	East Africa
Fila	FEE-lah	Badness	Swahili	East Africa

13

KENYA TANZANIA

Name	Pronunciation	Meaning	Origin	Region
Firdawsi	FEE-daw-SEE	Paradise beautiful garden	Swahili	East Africa
Firyali	FEE-yah-lee	Extraordinary	Swahili	East Africa
Freya	FREH-yah	Godess of love,	Swahili	East Africa
Fujo	FOO-joh	Born after parents' separation	Swahili	East Africa
Furaha	FOO-rah-hah	Happiness	Swahili	East Africa
Gasira	GAH-see-rah	Bold, courageous	Swahili	East Africa
Ghalyela	GIRL-yeh-lah	Expensive, precious	Swahili	East Africa
Ghanima	GAH-nee-mah	Good fortune	Swahili	East Africa
Gharibuu	Gah-ree-BOO	Stranger, visitor	Swahili	East Africa
Gheche	GEH-che	Small thing	Swahili	East Africa
Ghinjo	GHEE-nn-jo	Slaughter, cut	Swahili	East Africa
Ghipe	GHEE-peh	Sprout .	Swahili	East Africa
Habeebah	HAH-bee-bah	Dear one	Swahili	East Africa
Habiba	HAH-bee-bah	Beloved	Swahili	East Africa
Habibah	Hah-BEE-bah	Beloved	Swahili	East Africa
Hadhi	HAH-dee	Respect, honor	Swahili	East Africa
Hadiya	Hah-DEE-yah	Gift	Swahili	East Africa
Hafidha	HAH-fee-dah	Mindful	Swahili	East Africa
Hafsa	HAH-fhh-sah	Sound judgment	Swahili	East Africa
Haiba	HAH-ee-bah	Charm	Swahili	East Africa
Haifa.	HAH-ee-fah	Slim	Swahili	East Africa
Hakika	HAH-kee-kah	Truth	Swahili	East Africa
Hakima	Hah-kee-MAH	Sensible	Swahili	East Africa
Hala	HAH-lah	Glorious	Swahili	East Africa
Halili	HAH-lee-lee	Beloved one	Swahili	East Africa
Halima	Hah-LEE-mah	Gentle	Swahili	East Africa
Halisi	HAH-lee-see	Truth	Swahili	East Africa
Hamida	HAH-mee-dah	Gracious	Swahili	East Africa
Hanaa	HAH-nah-ah	Happiness	Swahili	East Africa
Hanifa	HAH-nee-fah	Pure	Swahili	East Africa

KENYA TANZANIA

Name	Pronunciation	Meaning	Origin	Region
Hanuni	HAH-noo-nee	Cheerful	Swahili	East Africa
Haoniyao	Hah-oh-nee-YAH-oh	Born at the time of a quarrel	Swahili	East Africa
Harbuu	HAH-boo	Warrior	Swahili	East Africa
Hartha	HAH-thaa	Arable, fertile	Swahili	East Africa
Hasanati	Hah-sah-NAH-tee	Good	Swahili	East Africa
Hashiki	HAH-she-kee	Passion	Swahili	East Africa
Hasijna	HAH-seej-nah	Beautiful, attractive	Swahili	East Africa
Hasina	Hah-SEE-nah	Good	Swahili	East Africa
Hasnaa	HAS-naa	Beauty	Swahili	East Africa
Hawa	HA-wah	Eve wife of Adam	Swahili	East Africa
Hawla	HAH-oo-lah	Graceful antelope	Swahili	East Africa
Hazina	HAH-zee-nah	Treasure	Swahili	East Africa
Hediye	HEH-dee-yeh	Gift	Swahili	East Africa
Hiarl	HEE-ah-ree	Free will	Swahili	East Africa
Hiba	Hee-BAH	Gift	Swahili	East Africa
Hidaya	Hee-DAH-yah	Precious gift	Swahili	East Africa
Himidi	HEE-mee-dee	All praises to God	Swahili	East Africa
Hisani	HEE-sah-nee	Kind, good-natured	Swahili	East Africa
Hissa	HEE-sah	Forgiveness, pardon	Swahili	East Africa
Hobo	HOH-boh	Gift	Swahili	East Africa
Horera	HO-reh-rah	Kitten	Swahili	East Africa
Huba	WHO-bah	Love, friendship	Swahili	East Africa
Hudham	WHO-dahm	Astute	Swahili	East Africa
Hun	WHO-nn	Free person	Swahili	East Africa
Huruma	WHO-roo-mah	Compassion, mercy	Swahili	East Africa
Hususa	WHO-soo-sah	Special	Swahili	East Africa
Ibtisam	Ee-beet-SAHM	Smile	Swahili	East Africa
Idihi	Ee-DEE	Enthusiasm, perseverance	Swahili	East Africa
Iffat	Ee-FAHT	Virtue	Swahili	East Africa

KENYA TANZANIA

Name	Pronunciation	Meaning	Origin	Region
Ilham	Eel-HAM	Inspiration	Swahili	East Africa
Imani	Ee-MAH-nee	Faith	Swahili	East Africa
Imani	Ee-MAH-nee	Faith	Swahili	East Africa
Imara	Ee-MAH-rah	Firm	Swahili	East Africa
Inaya	Ee-NAH-yah	Providence	Swahili	East Africa
Intisar	Eentee-sah	Victory	Swahili	East Africa
Itidal	Ee-tee-DAHL	Symmetry	Swahili	East Africa
Ituri	Ee-TOO-ree	Sweet-smelling	Swahili	East Africa
Jaha	JAH-hah	Dignity	Swahili	East Africa
Jahi	JAH-hee	Prominence	Swahili	East Africa
Jahia	JAH-hee-ah	Prominent	Swahili	East Africa
jali	JAH-lee	Respect, honor	Swahili	East Africa
jamala	JAH-mah-lah	Friendly, good manners	Swahili	East Africa
Jamila	Jah-MEE-lah	Beautiful	Swahili	East Africa
Jamila	Jah-MEE-lah	Beautiful	Swahili	East Africa
jana	JAH-nah	Healthy child/ Yesterday	Swahili	East Africa
Janna	JAH-nah	Heaven	Swahili	East Africa
Jasira	JAH-see-rah	Bold, courageous	Swahili	East Africa
Jauhar	JAH-ooh-hah	Jewel	Swahili	East Africa
Jina	GEE-nah	Name, identity	Swahili	East Africa
Jinaki	GEE-nah-key	Self-confident, proud	Swahili	East Africa
Jioni	GEE-oh-nee	Evening	Swahili	East Africa
Jirani	GEE-rah-nee	Neighbour	Swahili	East Africa
Johanna	JOH-hah-nah	God's grace	Swahili	East Africa
Johari	JOH-hah-ree	Something valuable	Swahili	East Africa
Jokha	JOH-kah	Robe of adornment	Swahili	East Africa
Joldia	JOH-kah	Robe of adornment	Swahili	East Africa
Judhar	JUU-dah	Uproot	Swahili	East Africa
Jumu	JUH-moo	Fate, luck	Swahili	East Africa

KENYA TANZANIA

Name	Pronunciation	Meaning	Origin	Region
Juwayria	JUH-wah-ree-yah	A damask rose	Swahili	East Africa
Juza	JUH-zah	Notify	Swahili	East Africa
Kabisa	KAH-bee-sah	For good	Swahili	East Africa
Kadija	Kah-DEE-jah	Wife of the Prophet Mohammed	Swahili	East Africa
Kalorii	KAH-loh-ree	Feeble	Swahili	East Africa
Kamaria	Kah-mah-REE-ah	Like the moon	Swahili	East Africa
Kamili	Kah-MEE-lee	Perfection	Swahili	East Africa
Kamilya	KAH-meel-yah	Perfection	Swahili	East Africa
Kanai	KAH-nah-ee	Contentment	Swahili	East Africa
Kanzi	KAHN-zee	A treasure	Swahili	East Africa
Karama	KAH-rah-mah	Honor, respect, esteem	Swahili	East Africa
Karamu	KAH-rah-moo	Precious gift	Swahili	East Africa
Karima	KAH-ree-mah	Generous	Swahili	East Africa
Karimu	Kah-REE-mu	Generous	Swahili	East Africa
Kashore	KAH-SHO-reh	With humor	Swahili	East Africa
Kauthar	KAH-ooh-thar	Abundant	Swahili	East Africa
Kawaida	KAH-wah-ee-dah	Natural	Swahili	East Africa
Kazija	KAH-zee-jah	Work comes	Swahili	East Africa
Kesi	KEH-see	Born at a time of father's troubles	Swahili	East Africa
Khadija	Kah-DEE-jah	Wife of the Prophet Mohammed	Swahili	East Africa
Khanfura	KAHN-foo-rah	Snort	Swahili	East Africa
Khola	Cola	Graceful antelope	Swahili	East Africa
Kiaga	KEE-ah-gah	Promise	Swahili	East Africa
Kianga	Kee-AHN-gah	Sunshine	Swahili	East Africa
Kibali	KEE-bah-lee	Favor	Swahili	East Africa
Kibibi	Kee-BEE-bee	Little lady	Swahili	East Africa
Kiburi	KEE-boo-ree	Pride	Swahili	East Africa

KENYA TANZANIA

Name	Pronunciation	Meaning	Origin	Region
Kidawa	KEE-dah-wah	Medicine	Swahili	East Africa
Kidhi	Kee-DEE	Satisfaction	Swahili	East Africa
Kifaa	Kee-FAAH	Useful	Swahili	East Africa
Kifimbo	Kee-FEEM-hoh	A delicate twig	Swahili	East Africa
Kijakazi	Kee-jah-KAH-zee	Your life is due to us	Swahili	East Africa
Kijicho	KEE-jee-cho	Envious, jealous	Swahili	East Africa
Kike	Kee-KEH	Feminine, femininity	Swahili	East Africa
Kimacho	KEE-mah-cho	Observant	Swahili	East Africa
Kinaya	KEE-nah-yah	Complete	Swahili	East Africa
Kinuka	KEE-noo-kah	A type of flower	Swahili	East Africa
Kinyemi	KEE-NYEH-mee	A good thing	Swahili	East Africa
Kioja	KEE-oh-jah	Miracle	Swahili	East Africa
Kipendo	KEE-pehn-doh	Love	Swahili	East Africa
Kipenzi	Kee-PEHN-zee	Loved one	Swahili	East Africa
Kipusa	KEE-poo-sah	Young girl	Swahili	East Africa
Kirafiki	KEE-rah-fee-kee	Like a friend	Swahili	East Africa
Kirimu	Kee-ree-muh	Generous, kind	Swahili	East Africa
Kisasa	Kee-sah-sah	New, modern	Swahili	East Africa
Kisima	Kee-see-MAH	Spring	Swahili	East Africa
Kitambi	Kee-tam-bee	Proud	Swahili	East Africa
Kito	Kee-toh	A jewel	Swahili	East Africa
Kitoto	Kee-toh-TOH	Precious child	Swahili	East Africa
Kizo	Kee-ZOH	An abundance	Swahili	East Africa
Kujuwakwangu	KOO-juh-wah-kwahn-goo	My knowledge	Swahili	East Africa
Kulula	KUH-loo-lah	Superior	Swahili	East Africa
Kupenda	Kuh-PEHN-duh	To love	Swahili	East Africa
Kurwa	Kuh-WAH	The second of two	Swahili	East Africa
Kwasi	KWAH-see	Wealthy	Swahili	East Africa
Kyesi	KYEH-see	Joy	Swahili	East Africa
Laini	LAH-ee-nee	Soft and gentle	Swahili	East Africa

18

KENYA TANZANIA

Name	Pronunciation	Meaning	Origin	Region
Lalamika	Lah-lah-mee-KAH	Pray for mercy	Swahili	East Africa
Lamia	LAH-mee-ah	Glitter	Swahili	East Africa
Latifa	LAH-tee-fah	Gentle	Swahili	East Africa
Latifah	LAH-tee-fah	Gentle	Swahili	East Africa
Latifu	LAH-tee-foo	Gentle	Swahili	East Africa
Layla	LAH-ee-lah	Born at night	Swahili	East Africa
Lela	LEH-lah	The night	Swahili	East Africa
Lila	LEE-lah	Good	Swahili	East Africa
Liwaza	LEE-wah-zah	Consolation	Swahili	East Africa
Lubaya	LOO-bah-yah	Young lioness	Swahili	East Africa
Lulu	LOO-loo	A pearl	Swahili	East Africa
Maarifa	MAAH-ree-fah	Skilled	Swahili	East Africa
Machui	MAH-choo-ee	Like a leopard	Swahili	East Africa
Madaha	Mah-DAH-hah	Graceful	Swahili	East Africa
Madiha	MAH-dee-hah	Worthy of praise	Swahili	East Africa
Mafunda	MAH-foon-dah	Teachings	Swahili	East Africa
Mahbuba	MAH-boo-bah	Beloved	Swahili	East Africa
Mahfudha	MAH-foo-dah	Protected	Swahili	East Africa
Maijani	Mahr-JAH-nee	Coral	Swahili	East Africa
Maimuna	MAH-ee-moo-nah	Blessed	Swahili	East Africa
Maisha	Mah-ee-SHAH	Life	Swahili	East Africa
Makini	Mah-KEE-nee	Calm and serene	Swahili	East Africa
Malaika	Mah-LAH-ee-kah	Angel	Swahili	East Africa
Malenga	MAH-lehn-gah	She sings well	Swahili	East Africa
Malia	MAH-lee-ah	Queen	Swahili	East Africa
Maliha	MAH-lee-hah	Pleasant	Swahili	East Africa
Malika	MAH-lee-kah	Queen	Swahili	East Africa
Maliwaza	Mah-lee-wah-zah	Consolation	Swahili	East Africa
Malkia	MAHL-kee-ah	Queen	Swahili	East Africa

KENYA TANZANIA

Name	Pronunciation	Meaning	Origin	Region
Maluum	MAA-loom	Special	Swahili	East Africa
Manga	MAHN-gah	Wanderer	Swahili	East Africa
Mapenzi	MAH-pehn-zee	Romance	Swahili	East Africa
Marashi	MAH-rah-shee	Fragrance, perfume	Swahili	East Africa
Mariamu	MAH-ree-ahm-oo	For the virgin Mary	Swahili	East Africa
Marini	MAH-ree-nee	Charming	Swahili	East Africa
Marjani	Mahr-JAH-nee	Coral	Swahili	East Africa
Masara	MAH-sah-rah	Joy	Swahili	East Africa
Mashavu	Mah-SHAH-vu	Chubby cheeks	Swahili	East Africa
Masika	Mah-SEE-kah	Born in the rainy season	Swahili	East Africa
Masiya	MAH-see-yah	Messiah	Swahili	East Africa
Maskini	Mah-SKEE-nee	Poor	Swahili	East Africa
Mastura	MAHS-too-rah	Without blemish	Swahili	East Africa
Mathna	MAH-thnah	Praise	Swahili	East Africa
Matima	MAH-tee-mah	Full moon	Swahili	East Africa
Matuko	MAH-too-koh	Elegance	Swahili	East Africa
Maua	MAH-oo-ah	Flowers	Swahili	East Africa
Maulidi	Mah-oo-LEE-dee	Born during Maulidi	Swahili	East Africa
Mayasa	MAH-yah-sah	Walks proudly	Swahili	East Africa
Maysara	MY-sah-rah	Ease	Swahili	East Africa
Mchumba	Mchoom-bah	Sweetheart	Swahili	East Africa
Mema	Meh-MAH	Goodness	Swahili	East Africa
Menikaliya	MEH-nee-kah-lee-yah	You are against me	Swahili	East Africa
Mera	MEH-rah	Mary	Swahili	East Africa
Meyya	MEH-yah	Mary	Swahili	East Africa
Meyye	MEH-yeh	Mary	Swahili	East Africa
Mgeni	M-GEH-nee	Visitor	Swahili	East Africa
Midra	MEE-drah	Princess	Swahili	East Africa
Midwa	M-KEE-wah	Orphaned child	Swahili	East Africa

KENYA TANZANIA

Name	Pronunciation	Meaning	Origin	Region
Mila	MEE-lah	Traditions	Swahili	East Africa
Milele	MEE-leh-leh	Eternity	Swahili	East Africa
Mimi	MEE-mee	I am	Swahili	East Africa
Mkali	M-KAH-lee	Fierce	Swahili	East Africa
Mkiyoni	M-KEE-yoh-nee	You don't see it	Swahili	East Africa
Mkweli	M-KWEH-lee	Truthful	Swahili	East Africa
Mmanga	M-man-gah	Make a journey	Swahili	East Africa
Monima	MOH-nee-mah	It is wrong to envy others	Swahili	East Africa
Mooza	MOO-ooh-zah	Sulky	Swahili	East Africa
Mosi	MOH-see	The first born	Swahili	East Africa
Moza	MOH-zah	Distinguished	Swahili	East Africa
Mpenzi	M-pehn-zee	Sweetheart	Swahili	East Africa
Mpingo	M-peen-GOH	Ebony	Swahili	East Africa
Mrashi	M-rah-shee	Rose water	Swahili	East Africa
Msaada	M-saah-dah	Assistance	Swahili	East Africa
Mshinda	M-sheen-dah	Who triumphs	Swahili	East Africa
Msiba	M-SEE-bah	Born during calamity or mourning	Swahili	East Africa
Mtakuja	M-tah-koo-jah	You will come	Swahili	East Africa
Mtakwishayenu	M-tah-kwee-shah-yeh-noo	You will exhaust yours	Swahili	East Africa
Mtama	M-tah-mah	Millet	Swahili	East Africa
Mtumwa	M-too-mwah	Servant	Swahili	East Africa
Mtupeni	M-too-PEH-nee	Not very welcome	Swahili	East Africa
Mua	MOOH-ah	Healing, benefit	Swahili	East Africa
Mufiida	MOO-fee-dah	Beneficial	Swahili	East Africa
Muhima	MUH-hee-mah	Of importance	Swahili	East Africa
Muna	MUH-nah	Hope	Swahili	East Africa
Munira	MUH-nee-rah	Radiant	Swahili	East Africa
Murua	Moo-ROO-ah	Elegant and refined	Swahili	East Africa

KENYA TANZANIA

Name	Pronunciation	Meaning	Origin	Region
Muslima	MOOH-slee-mah	One who submits to God	Swahili	East Africa
Mvita	M-vee-tah	Full of life	Swahili	East Africa
Mwajuma	M-wah-JOO-mah	Born on Friday	Swahili	East Africa
Mwaka	M-WAH-kah	Born at the year's opening	Swahili	East Africa
Mwamini	M-wah-MEE-nee	Honest one	Swahili	East Africa
Mwammoja	MWAH-m-moh-jah	The only one	Swahili	East Africa
Mwana	MWAH-nah	Lady	Swahili	East Africa
Mwanabaraka	MWAH-nah-bah-rah-kah	Brings blessings	Swahili	East Africa
Mwanadongo	MWAH-nah-dohn-goh	Child of the earth	Swahili	East Africa
Mwanahamisi	M-wah-nah-hah-MEE-see	Born on Thursday	Swahili	East Africa
Mwanahawa	MWAH-nah-hawa	Daughter of Eve	Swahili	East Africa
Mwanaidi	M-wah-nah-EE-dee	Born during the Idd festival	Swahili	East Africa
Mwanajuma	M-wah-nah-JOO-mah	Born on Friday	Swahili	East Africa
Mwanakhamisi	M-wah-nah-hah-MEE-see	Born on Thursday	Swahili	East Africa
Mwanakheri	MWAH-nah-HEH-ree	Brings goodness	Swahili	East Africa
Mwanakweli	MWAH-nah-kweh-lee	Brings truth	Swahili	East Africa
Mwanamize	MWAH-nah-mee-zeh	Distinguished	Swahili	East Africa
Mwanatabu	M-wah-nah-TAH-boo	Born at time of trouble	Swahili	East Africa
Mwari	MWAH-re	A girl who has reached puberty	Swahili	East Africa

22

KENYA TANZANIA

Name	Pronunciation	Meaning	Origin	Region
Mwasaa	M-wa-SAH	Timely	Swahili	East Africa
Mwasham	MWAH-shahm	Unlucky	Swahili	East Africa
Mwatabu	M-wah-TAH-boo	Born at a time of sorrow	Swahili	East Africa
Mwema	MWEH-mah	Good	Swahili	East Africa
Mzuri	M-zuh-ree	I feel good	Swahili	East Africa
Nabila	NAH-bee-la	Noble	Swahili	East Africa
Nadhari	NAH-tha-ree	Vision	Swahili	East Africa
Nadhiri	NAH-thee-ree	Vow	Swahili	East Africa
Nadia	NAH-dee-ah	Caller	Swahili	East Africa
Nadiya	NAH-dee-yah	Generous	Swahili	East Africa
Nadra	NAH-drah	Unique	Swahili	East Africa
Nafaika	NAH-fah-ee-kah	Prosperity	Swahili	East Africa
Nafasi	NAH-fah-see	Opportunity	Swahili	East Africa
Nafia	Nah-FEE-ah	Gift	Swahili	East Africa
Nafisa	NAH-fee-sah	Precious gem	Swahili	East Africa
Nafisi	NAH-fee-see	To save	Swahill	East Africa
Nafisika	NAH-fee-see-kah	Well to do	Swahili	East Africa
Naima	NAH-ee-mah	Graceful	Swahili	East Africa
Najaat	NAH-jah-t	Safety	Swahili	East Africa
Najah	NAH-jah	Success	Swahili	East Africa
Najia	NAH-jee-ah	Progeny	Swahili	East Africa
Najma	NAH-jh-mah	Star	Swahili	East Africa
Najya	NAH-jyah	Saved	Swahili	East Africa
Nakawa	NAH-kah-wah	Beautiful	Swahili	East Africa
Nana	NAH-nah	Lady	Swahili	East Africa
Nasiim	NAH-seem	Fresh air	Swahili	East Africa
Nasra	NAH-srah	Assistance	Swahili	East Africa
Natasa	NAH-tah-sah	Skillful	Swahili	East Africa
Nathari	NAH-thah-ree	Prose	Swahili	East Africa
Nawiri	NAH-wee-ree	Healthy	Swahili	East Africa

KENYA TANZANIA

Name	Pronunciation	Meaning	Origin	Region
Nayfa	NAI-fah	Benefit	Swahili	East Africa
Nayla	NAI-lah	Gain	Swahili	East Africa
Naysun	NAY-soon	Seedless grapes	Swahili	East Africa
Nazura	NAH-zuh-rah	Foremost	Swahili	East Africa
Ndege	N-deh-GEH	Bird	Swahili	East Africa
Neema	Neh-EH-mah	Born in times of prosperity	Swahili	East Africa
Neemaka	Nee-MAH-kah	Benevolent	Swahili	East Africa
Nena	NEH-nah	Speak	Swahili	East Africa
Nia	NEE-ah	Intention, purpose	Swahili	East Africa
Niara	NEE-ah-rah	Of high purpose	Swahili	East Africa
Nina	NEE-nah	Mother	Swahili	East Africa
Nishati	NEE-shah-tee	Full of vigor	Swahili	East Africa
Njema	JEH-mah	Good	Swahili	East Africa
Noni	NOH-nee	Gift of God	Swahili	East Africa
Nteremezi	N-tereh-meh-zee	Cheerful person	Swahili	East Africa
Nuaha	NUH-ah-ah	Pleasure	Swahili	East Africa
Nufaika	NUH-fah-ee-kah	Prosperity	Swahili	East Africa
Nuha	NUH-hah	Consoled	Swahili	East Africa
Nunuu	NUH-nuu	Extol	Swahili	East Africa
Nura	NUH-rah	Bnghtness	Swahili	East Africa
Nurisha	NUH-ree-shah	Shine light upon	Swahili	East Africa
Nuru	Noo-ROO	In the daylight	Swahili	East Africa
Nusurika	NUH-soo-ree-kah	Saved from difficulty	Swahili	East Africa
Nyemya	NYEH-meh-yah	Self-esteem	Swahili	East Africa
Nyimbo	NYEHM-boh	Song	Swahili	East Africa
Nyofu	NYOH-fuu	Candid	Swahili	East Africa
Paka	PAH-kah	Cat	Swahili	East Africa
Panya	PAHN-yah	Mouse (a tiny baby)	Swahili	East Africa

KENYA TANZANIA

Name	Pronunciation	Meaning	Origin	Region
Pasua	Pah-SOO-ah	Born by Caesarean operation	Swahili	East Africa
Patanisha	PAH-tah-nee-shah	Reconcile	Swahili	East Africa
Pendo	PEHN-doh	Love	Swahili	East Africa
Penzima	PEHN-zee-mah	Desire	Swahili	East Africa
Pili	PEE-lee	The second born	Swahili	East Africa
Pulika	POOH-lee-kah	Obedience	Swahili	East Africa
Raawiya	RAAH-wee-yah	Story teller	Swahili	East Africa
Rabia	RAH-bee-ah	Spring	Swahili	East Africa
Rabuwa	RAH-booh-wah	Grow	Swahili	East Africa
Radhi	RAH-dee	Forgiveness	Swahili	East Africa
Rafiya	RAH-fee-yah	Dignified	Swahili	East Africa
Rahima	Rah-hee-MAH	Compassionate	Swahili	East Africa
Rahimu	RAH-hee-moo	Mercy	Swahili	East Africa
Rahma	RAH-mah	Compassion	Swahili	East Africa
Raisa	Rah-ee-SAH	Exalted	Swahili	East Africa
Ramla	RAHM-lah	Predictor of the future	Swahili	East Africa
Rayha	RAY-hah	A little luxury	Swahili	East Africa
Rayyan	RAY-ahn	Luxuriant, lush	Swahili	East Africa
Razina	Rah-zee-NAH	Strong and patient	Swahili	East Africa
Raziya	Rah-ZEE-yah	Agreeable	Swahili	East Africa
Reem	Reem	White antelope	Swahili	East Africa
Rehani	Reh-HAH-nee	Promise	Swahili	East Africa
Rehema	Reh-HEH-mah	Compassion	Swahili	East Africa
Remba	Reh-m-BAH	Beautiful	Swahili	East Africa
Ridhaa	Ree-DAAH	Goodwill	Swahili	East Africa
Ridhisha	REE-dee-shah	Satisfaction	Swahili	East Africa
Rim	Reem	White antelope	Swahili	East Africa
Riziki	REE-zee-kee	Daily sustenance	Swahili	East Africa
Rozi	ROH-zee	Flower, rose	Swahili	East Africa

KENYA TANZANIA

Name	Pronunciation	Meaning	Origin	Region
Rukiya	Roo-KEE-yah	She rises high	Swahili	East Africa
Ruqaya	Rooh-KWAH-yah	Superior	Swahili	East Africa
Ruzuna	Rooh-zoo-NAH	Calm and composed	Swahili	East Africa
Saada	Sah-AH-dah	Helper	Swahili	East Africa
Saadiya	SAAH-dee-yah	Happy	Swahili	East Africa
Sabiha	SAH-bee-HAH	Graceful	Swahili	East Africa
Sabir	SAH-beer	Patient	Swahili	East Africa
Sabra	SAH-brah	Patience	Swahili	East Africa
Saburi	SAH-boo-ree	Patience	Swahili	East Africa
Sadaka	SAH-dah-kah	An offering	Swahili	East Africa
Sadiki	SAH-dee-kee	Believable	Swahili	East Africa
Sadikifu	SAH-dee-kee-fu	Reliable friend	Swahili	East Africa
Sadikika	SAH-dee-kee-kah	Trustworthy	Swahili	East Africa
Safaa	Sah-FAH	Purity	Swahili	East Africa
Safi	SAH-fee	Pure	Swahili	East Africa
Safidi	SAH-fee-dee	Well organized, tidy	Swahili	East Africa
Safisha	Sah-FEE-shah	Cleansing	Swahili	East Africa
Safiya	Sah-FEE-yah	Clear-minded, pure	Swahili	East Africa
Saida	SAH-ee-dah	Happy	Swahili	East Africa
Saiha	SAH-ee-hah	Good	Swahili	East Africa
Saiwa	Sah-ee-WAH	Consolation	Swahili	East Africa
Sakina	SAH-kee-NAH	Tranquility calm	Swahili	East Africa
Sala	Sah-LAH	Prayer	Swahili	East Africa
Salama	Sah-LAH-mah	Peace	Swahili	East Africa
Salamu	Sah-LAH-moo	Perfect	Swahili	East Africa
Salima	Sah-lee-MAH	Safe	Swahili	East Africa
Salma	SAHL-mah	Safe	Swahili	East Africa
Salme	Sahl-meh	Safe	Swahili	East Africa
Samiha	Sah-MEE-hah	Magnanimous	Swahili	East Africa
Samira	Sah-MEE-rah	Reconciler	Swahili	East Africa

KENYA TANZANIA

Name	Pronunciation	Meaning	Origin	Region
Sanaa	SAH-naa	Art	Swahili	East Africa
Sanura	Sah-NOO-rah	Kitten	Swahili	East Africa
Sauda	Sah-OO-dah	Dark beauty	Swahili	East Africa
Saumu	SAH-oo-muh	Born during Ramadan	Swahili	East Africa
Sauti	SAH-oo-tee	Voice	Swahili	East Africa
Sebtuu	SEHB-tuu	Born on Saturday	Swahili	East Africa
Semeni	SEH-meh-nee	Speak	Swahili	East Africa
Shahida	Shah-hee-DAH	Martyr	Swahili	East Africa
Shakila	Shah-KEE-lah	Shapely	Swahili	East Africa
Shamba	Shah-m-BAH	Plantation	Swahili	East Africa
Shamim	Shah-MEEM	Sweet scent	Swahili	East Africa
Shangilia	Shahn-GEE-lah	Celebrate	Swahili	East Africa
Shangwe	Shahn-GWEH	Celebration	Swahili	East Africa
Shani	SHAH-nee	Marvellous	Swahili	East Africa
Sharifa	Shah-REE-fah	Distinguished one	Swahili	East Africa
Shawana	Shah-WAH-nah	Grace	Swahili	East Africa
Shemsa	SHEHM-sah	Sunlight	Swahili	East Africa
Sheshe	SHEH-sheh	Elegance	Swahili	East Africa
Shiba	SHEE-bah	Satiated	Swahili	East Africa
Shida	SHEE-dah	Difficulty	Swahili	East Africa
Shifaa	SHEE-fah	Cure	Swahili	East Africa
Shirika	SHEE-ree-kah	Trusted partner	Swahili	East Africa
Shukura	Shoo-KOO-rah	I am grateful	Swahili	East Africa
Shukuru	Shoo-koo-ROO	Grateful	Swahili	East Africa
Shuruku	Shoo-roo-KOO	Dawn	Swahili	East Africa
Sibadili	SEE-bah-dee-lee	I will not change	Swahili	East Africa
Sihaba	SEE-hah-bah	Not a little	Swahili	East Africa
Siham	SEE-hahm	Sharing together	Swahili	East Africa
Sijaona	SEE-jah-oh-nah	I have not seen	Swahili	East Africa
Sikia	SEE-kee-ah	Harmony	Swahili	East Africa
Sikitu	SEE-kee-too	It's all right	Swahili	East Africa

KENYA TANZANIA

Name	Pronunciation	Meaning	Origin	Region
Sikudhani	See-koo-THAH-nee	A pleasant suprise	Swahili	East Africa
Silika	SEE-lee-kah	Instinct	Swahili	East Africa
Siri	See-ree	Secret	Swahili	East Africa
Sisya	SEE-s-yah	She of the Mfuu tree	Swahili	East Africa
Siti	SEE-tee	Lady	Swahili	East Africa
Siwatu	See- WAH-too	Born during time of conflict with another	Swahili	East Africa
Siwazuri	See-wah-ZOO-ree	Those people are not good	Swahili	East Africa
Siyasa	See-YAH-sah	A politician	Swahili	East Africa
Somo	Soh-MOH	Teachings or godmother	Swahili	East Africa
Somoe	Soh-MOH-eh	Her godmother	Swahili	East Africa
Staajabu	S-TAAH-jah-boo	Amazement	Swahili	East Africa
Stara	S-TAH-rah	Protected	Swahili	East Africa
Subira	Soo-BEE-rah	The reward of patience	Swahili	East Africa
Suhaila	Soo-HAH-ee-lah	Ease	Swahili	East Africa
Suluma	SOO-loo-mah	Security	Swahili	East Africa
Sumaiyya	Soo-MAH-ee-yah	Of good reputation	Swahili	East Africa
Surayya	Soo-rah-ee-yah	Noble	Swahili	East Africa
Taabu	Tah-AH-boo	Troubles	Swahili	East Africa
Tabasamu	TAH-bah-sah-mu	A beautiful smile	Swahili	East Africa
Tabia	Tah-BEE-ah	Good conduct	Swahili	East Africa
Tabita	TAH-bee-tah	Graceful	Swahili	East Africa
Tafida	TAH-fee-dah	Benefit	Swahili	East Africa
Tahira	TAH-hee-rah	Dean	Swahili	East Africa
Tahiya	TAH-hee-yah	Security	Swahili	East Africa
Talha	TAHL-hah	Easy life	Swahili	East Africa
Tamaa	Tah-MAA	Desire	Swahili	East Africa

KENYA TANZANIA

Name	Pronunciation	Meaning	Origin	Region
Tamasha	Tah-MAH-shah	Happy occasion	Swahili	East Africa
Tambika	Tahm-BEE-kah	Offering	Swahili	East Africa
Tambuzi	TAHM-boo-zee	Intelligent	Swahili	East Africa
Tamu	TAH-moo	Sweet	Swahili	East Africa
Tanabahi	Tah-NAH-bah-ee	Be cautious	Swahili	East Africa
Tanashati	Tah-NAH-shah-tee	Well dressed and neat	Swahili	East Africa
Taraji	Tah-RAH-jee	Hope, faith	Swahili	East Africa
Tarajika	Tah-RAH-jee-KAH	Hope, faith	Swahili	East Africa
Tathinina	TAH-thee-nee-nah	High value	Swahili	East Africa
Tatu	TAH-too	Third born	Swahili	East Africa
Tawa	TAH-wah	A religious person	Swahili	East Africa
Tefle	TEH-fleh	Infancy, beginning	Swahili	East Africa
Terema	TEH-reh-mah	A cheerful person	Swahili	East Africa
Time	TEE-meh	Full of happiness	Swahili	East Africa
Tisha	TEE-shah	Strong-willed	Swahili	East Africa
Tosha	TOH-shah	Satisfaction	Swahili	East Africa
Tufaha	Too-FAH-hah	Apple	Swahili	East Africa
Tuhfa	Too-FAH	A gift	Swahili	East Africa
Tumaini	Too-MAH-ee-nee	Hope	Swahili	East Africa
Tuni	TOO-nee	Tune	Swahili	East Africa
Tunu	TOO-nooh	Novelty	Swahili	East Africa
Turkiya	TOO-kee-yah	Beautiful	Swahili	East Africa
Uheri	Oo-HEH-ree	Good fortune	Swahili	East Africa
Ujamaa	Oo-JAH-mah	Family	Swahili	East Africa
Ukarimu	Oo-KAH-ree-moo	Hospitality	Swahili	East Africa
Unguja	Oon-goo-JAH	Zanzibar	Swahili	East Africa
Uzima	Oo-zee-MAH	Energetic, vitality	Swahili	East Africa

KENYA TANZANIA

Name	Pronunciation	Meaning	Origin	Region
Uzuri	Oo-zoo-ree	Beauty	Swahili	East Africa
Waseme	Wah-SEH-meh	Let them talk	Swahili	East Africa
Wema	WEH-mah	Virtue goodness	Swahili	East Africa
Wepesi	WEH-peh-see	Swift	Swahili	East Africa
Wimbo	Weem-BOH	Song	Swahili	East Africa
Wingu	Ween-GUU	Heavenly cloud	Swahili	East Africa
Yakini	YAH-kee-nee	Truth	Swahili	East Africa
Yasmin	YAHS-meen	Jasmine	Swahili	East Africa
Yumna	YUHM-nah	Good luck	Swahili	East Africa
Yusra	YUHS-rah	Ease	Swahili	East Africa
Zaafarani	ZAAH-fah-rah-nee	Saffron	Swahili	East Africa
Zahra	ZAH-rah	Blossom	Swahili	East Africa
Zaida	Zah-ee-DAH	Abundance	Swahili	East Africa
Zaina	Zah-ee-NAH	Beautiful	Swahili	East Africa
Zainabu	ZAH-ee-nah-buh	Prophet Muhammad's daughter	Swahili	East Africa
Zainabu	Zah-ee-NAH-boo	Beautiful	Swahili	East Africa
Zaituni	Zaa-ee-TOO-nee	Olive, guava	Swahili	East Africa
Zakiya	Zah-KEE-yah	Intelligent	Swahili	East Africa
Zalika	Zah-LEE-kah	Well-born	Swahili	East Africa
Zalira	ZAH-rah	Flower	Swahili	East Africa
Zamani	Zah-MAH-nee	Long time ago	Swahili	East Africa
Zamzam	ZAHM-zahm	Holy spring	Swahili	East Africa
Zarifa	ZAH-ree-fah	Graceful	Swahili	East Africa
Zarina	ZAH-ree-nah	Golden	Swahili	East Africa
Zawadi	Zah-WAH-dee	Gift	Swahili	East Africa
Zaynab	ZAH-ee-NAH-b	Beautiful	Swahili	East Africa
Zena	ZEH-nah	Beautiful ornament	Swahili	East Africa
Zenabu	ZEH-nah-BOO	Beautiful	Swahili	East Africa

KENYA TANZANIA

Name	Pronunciation	Meaning	Origin	Region
Zera	ZEH-rah	Beauty, blooms, dawn	Swahili	East Africa
Zeyana	ZEH-yah-nah	Ornament	Swahili	East Africa
Zina	ZEE-nah	A beauty	Swahili	East Africa
Zubayda	ZUH-bay-dah	The best of all	Swahili	East Africa
Zubeda	ZUH-beh-dah	The best one	Swahili	East Africa
Zuhura	ZUH-hu-rah	Brightness, Venus	Swahili	East Africa
Zulaykha	ZUH-lay-kah	Brilliant one	Swahili	East Africa
Zulekha	ZUH-leh-kah	Brilliant one	Swahili	East Africa
Zuri	ZUH-ree	Beautiful, georgeous	Swahili	East Africa
Zuwena	Zoo-WEH-nah	Good	Swahili	East Africa

MALAWI

Name	Pronunciation	Meaning	Origin	Region
Abikanile	Ah-bee-kah-nee-lay	Listen	Yao	South Africa
Alile	Ah-LEE-leh	She weeps	Yao	South Africa
Asale	Ah-SAH-leh	Speak	Yao	South Africa
Buseje	Boo-SEH-jeh	Ask me	Yao	South Africa
Chaonaine	Chah-oh-nah-EE-neh	It has seen me	Ngoni	South Africa
Chifundo	Chee-foo-ndo	Mercy	Chichewa	South Africa
Chikondi	Chee-ko-ndi	Love	Chichewa	South Africa
Chimwala	Cheem-WAH-lah	Stone	Yao	South Africa
Chiwa	CHEF-wah	Death	Yao	South Africa
Chotsani	Chot-SAH-nee	Take away	Yao	South Africa
Dziko	ZEE-koh	The world	Ngoni	South Africa
Kantayeni	Kan-tah-YAY-nee	Go and throw her away	Yao	South Africa
Kausiwa	Kah-oo-SEE-wah	The poor	Yao	South Africa
Kuliraga	Koo-lee-RAH-gah	Weeping	Yao	South Africa

MALAWI

Name	Pronunciation	Meaning	Origin	Region
Kwasausya	Kwa-sah-OOS-yah	Troubled	Yao	South Africa
Liziuzayani	Lee-zee-OO-zah-YAH-nee	Tell someone	Yao	South Africa
Mabuufo	Mah-BOO-frh	Troubles	Ngoni	South Africa
Mesi	MEH-see	Water	Yao	South Africa
Mpatuleni	M-pah-too-LAY-nee	Separate	Ngoni	South Africa
Ndachitanji	N-aah-chee-TAN-jee	What have I done?	Ngoni	South Africa
Ngulinga	N-goo-LEEN-gah	Weeping	Ngoni	South Africa
Njemile	N-jeh-MEE-leh	Upstanding	Yao	South Africa
Sigele	See-GEH-leh	Left	Ngoni	South Africa
Tamanda	Ta-man-da	Worship	Chichewa	South Africa
Teleza	Teh-LEH-zah	Slippery	Ngoni	South Africa
Tidyanawo	Teed-yah-NAH-woh	We shall both eat	Ngoni	South Africa
Tisaubiranji	Ti-sah-oo-boo-RAN-jee	Why such poverty?	Ngoni	South Africa
Tithandianasi	Tee-tan-dee-ah-NAH-see	We'll be finished by relative	Ngoni	South Africa
Tiyamike	Tee-ya-mee-keh	Let us give thanks	Chichewa	South Africa

NIGERIA

Name	Pronounciation	Meaning	Origin	Region
Abayomi	Ah-BAH-yoh-mee	Pleasant meeting	Yoruba	West Africa
Abebi	AH-beh-BEE	We asked for her	Yoruba	West Africa
Abegbe	AH-bah-beh	We begged to have this one to lift up	Yoruba	West Africa

32

NIGERIA

Name	Pronounciation	Meaning	Origin	Region
Abeje	Ah-beh-JEH	We asked to have this one	Yoruba	West Africa
Abeke	Ah-beh-KEH	We begged for her to pet her	Yoruba	West Africa
Abeni	Ah-beh-NEE	We asked for her, and she is ours	Yoruba	West Africa
Abeo	Ah-beh-OH	Her birth brings happiness	Yoruba	West Africa
Abidemi	Ah-bee-deh-MEE	Born during father's absence	Yoruba	West Africa
Abimbola	Ah-BEEM-boh-lah	Born to be rich	Yoruba	West Africa
Abisola	Ah-bee-saw-la	Born into wealth	Yoruba	West Africa
Adebola	Ah-DEH-boh-lah	She met honor	Yoruba	West Africa
Adebomi	Ah-deh-bon-MEE	Crown covered my nakedness	Yoruba	West Africa
Adedewe	Ah-DEH-deh-weh	The crown is shattered	Yoruba	West Africa
Adedoja	Ah-DEH-doh-jah	Crown becomes a thing of worth	Yoruba	West Africa
Adeleke	Ah-DEH-leh-keh	Crown achieves happiness	Yoruba	West Africa
Adenrele	Ah-Dey-n-Ray-Lay	The crown has headed home to roost	Yoruba	West Africa
Adeola	Ah-deh-oh-LAH	Crown has honor	Yoruba	West Africa
Aderinola	Ah-DEH-ree-noh-lah	Crown walked toward wealth	Yoruba	West Africa

NIGERIA

Name	Pronounciation	Meaning	Origin	Region
Adesimbo	Ah-deh-SEEM-boh	Noble birth	Yoruba	West Africa
Adeyemi	Har dey yeh mi	Crown fits me	YORUBA	West Africa
Adia	AH-dee-ah	A gift	Hausa	West Africa
Aduke	Ah-doo-KEH	Much loved	Yoruba	West Africa
Aina	Ah-ee-NAH	Difficult birth	Yoruba	West Africa
Aiyetoro	Ah-YEH-toh-roh	Peace on earth	Yoruba	West Africa
Akanke	Ah-kahn-KEH	To meet her is to love her	Yoruba	West Africa
Alaba	Ah-lah-BAH	Second child born after twins	Yoruba	West Africa
Alake	Ah-lah-KEH	One to be petted and made much of	Yoruba	West Africa
Ama	Ah-MAH	Delivery had problems	Yoruba	West Africa
Amadi	Ah-MAH-dee	General rejoicing	Ibo	West Africa
Amonke	Ah-mohn-KEH	To know her is to pet her	Yoruba	West Africa
Areta	Ah-REH-tah	A charmer	Bini	West Africa
Arria	Ah-REE-ah	Slender	Hausa	West Africa
Asabi	Ah-sah-BEE	She is of choice birth	Yoruba	West Africa
Auta	Ah-OO-tah	The last born	Hausa	West Africa
Ayo	AH-yoh	Great joy	Yoruba	West Africa
Ayobami	Ah-yoh-BAH-mee	I am blessed with joy	Yoruba	West Africa
Ayobunmi	Ah-yoh-BOON-mee	Joy is given to me	Yoruba	West Africa
Ayodele	Ah-yoh-DEH-leh	Joy come home	Yoruba	West Africa
Ayofemi	Ah-yoh-FEH-mee	Joy likes me	Yoruba	West Africa

NIGERIA

Name	Pronounciation	Meaning	Origin	Region
Ayoluwa	Ah-yo-LOO-wah	Joy of our people	Yoruba	West Africa
Ayoola	Ah-YOH-oh-lah	Joy in wealth	Yoruba	West Africa
Azalee	Ah-zah-LEE	A singer	Bini	West Africa
Baderinwa	Bah-day-REEN-wah	Worthy of respect	Yoruba	West Africa
Baina	Bah-EE-nah	Sparkling	Bobangi	West Africa
Bayo	BAH-yoh	Joy is found	Yoruba	West Africa
Becca	BEH-cah	Prophet	Bobangi	West Africa
Bejide	Beh-JEE-deh	Child born in the rainy time	Yoruba	West Africa
Binah	BEE-nah	A dancer	Bobangi	West Africa
Bolade	BOH-lah-deh	Honor arrives	Yoruba	West Africa
Bolanile	Baw-lah-NEE-leh	The wealth of this house	Yoruba	West Africa
Bunmi	BOON-mee	My gift	Yoruba	West Africa
Chinue	CHEEN-weh	God's blessing	Ibo	West Africa
Chioma	Chee-o-ma	God's gift	Igbo	West Africa
Chisom	Chi so m	God is with me	Igbo	West Africa
Dada	DAH-dah	Child with curly hair	Yoruba	West Africa
Danuwa	Dah-NOO-wah	Close friend	Hausa	West Africa
Daurama	Dah-oo-RAH-mah	Ninth in the succession of queens	Hausa	West Africa
Dayo	DAH-yo	Joy arrives	Yoruba	West Africa
Ebun	Eh-BOON	Gift	Yoruba	West Africa
Edenausegboye	Eh-deh-nah-oo-seh-BOH-yeh	Good deeds are remembered	Benin	West Africa
Ehizemen	Eh-Hee-zemen	God's choice	Edo	West Africa
Ekaghogho	Eh-kah-HO-hoh	Born on an important day	Benin	West Africa

NIGERIA

Name	Pronounciation	Meaning	Origin	Region
Ekenesenarhienrhien	E-Ke-ne-se-nar-hien-rhien	Appreciate what God has given	Edo	West Africa
Enomwoyi	Eh-nohm-WOH-yee	One who has grace, charm	Benin	West Africa
Esosa	E so sa	God's blessing	Edo	West Africa
Etinosa	Ety-no-sah	God's power	Edo	West Africa
Fabayo	Fa-BAH-yoh	A lucky birth is joy	Yoruba	West Africa
Faraa	Fah-RAH	Cheerful one	Hausa	West Africa
Farih	Fah-REE	Bright and fair	Hausa	West Africa
Fayola	Fah-YOH-lah	Good fortune walks with honor	Yoruba	West Africa
Femi	FEH-mee	Love me	Yoruba	West Africa
Fola	FAW-lah	Honor	Yoruba	West Africa
Folade	Faw-lah-DEH	Honor arrives	Yoruba	West Africa
Folami	Faw-LAH-mee	Respect and honor me	Yoruba	West Africa
Folashade	Faw-lah-shah-DEH	Honor confers a crown	Yoruba	West Africa
Folayan	Faw-LAH-yahn	To walk in dignity	Yoruba	West Africa
Foluke	Foh-LOO-keh	Placed in God's care	Yoruba	West Africa
Gerda	GAYR-dah	Charmer of serpents	Hausa	West Africa
Gimbya	Geem-BEE-yah	Princess	Hausa	West Africa
Hanna	HAH-nah	Happiness	Hausa	West Africa
Hazika	Ha-ZEE-kah	Intelligent one	Hausa	West Africa
Hembadoon	HEM-bah-doon	The winner	Yoruba	West Africa
Idowu	Ee-doh-WOO	First child born after twins	Yoruba	West Africa

NIGERIA

Name	Pronounciation	Meaning	Origin	Region
Ifama	Ee-FAH-mah	All is well	Ibo	West Africa
Ife	Ee-FEH	Love	Yoruba	West Africa
Ifetayo	Ee-feh-TAH-yph	Love brings happiness	Yoruba	West Africa
Ige	EE-geh	Delivered feet first	Yoruba	West Africa
Ijaba	Ee-JAH-bah	A wish fulfilled	Hausa	West Africa
Ikuseghan	Ee-KOO-seh-han	Peace surpasses war	Benin	West Africa
Ina	EE-nah	Mother of the rains	Hausa	West Africa
Irawagbon	Ee-rah-WAH-bon	Enemy's attempt to kill her	Benin	West Africa
Isoke	Ee-SOH-keh	A satisfying gift from God	Benin	West Africa
Iverem	Ee-VEH-rem	Blessings and favors	Tiv	West Africa
Iyabo	Ee-YAH-boh	Mother has returned	Yoruba	West Africa
Izegbe	Ee-ZEH-beh	Long expected child	Benin	West Africa
Jumoke	Joo-MOH-keh	Everyone loves the child	Yoruba	West Africa
Kehinde	Keh-heen-DEH	Second born of twins	Yoruba	West Africa
Kinah	Kee-NAH	Willful	Bobangi	West Africa
Kiziah	Kee-ZEE-ah	Light hearted	Bini	West Africa
Kokumo	KOH-koo-moh	This one will not die	Yoruba	West Africa
Limber	LIM-ber	Joyfulness	Tiv	West Africa
Lina	LEE-nah	Tender	Hausa	West Africa
Lisha	LEE-shah	Mysterious	Hausa	West Africa
Iyabo	Ee-YAH-boh	Mother has returned	Yoruba	West Africa

NIGERIA

Name	Pronounciation	Meaning	Origin	Region
Mbafor	M-BAH-fohr	Born on a market day	Ibo	West Africa
Mbeke	M-beh-KEH	Born on the first day of the week	Ibo	West Africa
Mhonum	M-HOH-num	Mercifulness	Tiv	West Africa
Modupe	Moh-DOO-peh	I am grateful	Yoruba	West Africa
Monifa	MOH-nee-fah	I have my luck	Yoruba	West Africa
Morihinze	Moh-ree-hin-ZEH	Child of either sex is good	Tiv	West Africa
Nayo	NAH-yoh	We have great joy	Yoruba	West Africa
Nayo	NAH-yoh	We have joy	Yoruba	West Africa
Ngozi	N-GOH-zee	Blessing	Ibo	West Africa
Nkiruka	En-kee-roo-ka	The Future is Bright	Igbo	West Africa
Nneka	N-NEH-kah	Her mother is prominent	Ibo	West Africa
Nnenaya	Neh-NAH-yah	Like father's mother	Ibo	West Africa
Nnenia	N-NEH-nee-ah	Her grandmother's look alike	Ibo	West Africa
Nourbese	Noor-BEH-seh	A wonderful child	Benin	West Africa
Nwakaego	N-wah-kah-EH-goh	More important than money	Ibo	West Africa
Ode	Oh-DEH	Born along the road	Benin	West Africa
Ofure	Oh-Foo-Rah	Peace	Edo	West Africa
Olaniyi	Oh-lah-NEE-yee	There's glory in wealth	Yoruba	West Africa
Olabisi	Oh-LAH-bee-see	Joy is multiplied	Yoruba	West Africa

38

NIGERIA

Name	Pronounciation	Meaning	Origin	Region
Olabunmi	Aw-lah-BOON-mee	Honor has rewarded me	Yoruba	West Africa
Olaniyi	Oh-lah-NEE-yee	There's glory in wealth	Yoruba	West Africa
Olateju	Or-lah- teh ju	Abundant and renowned wealth	YORUBA	West Africa
Olubayo	Oh-loo-BAH-yoh	Greatest joy	Yoruba	West Africa
Olubunmi	Oh-loo-BOON-mee	God gave me	Yoruba	West Africa
Olufemi	Oh-LOO-feh-mee	God loves me	Yoruba	West Africa
Olufemi	O-loo-Fem-hi	God loves me	Yoruba	West Africa
Olufunke	Oh-loo-FOON-keh	God gives me to be loved	Yoruba	West Africa
Olufunmilayo	Oh-loo-foon-mee-LAH-yoh	God gives me joy	Yoruba	West Africa
Oluremi	Oh-loo-REH-mee	God consoles me	Yoruba	West Africa
Omolara	Oh-MOH-lah-rah	Born at the right time	Benin	West Africa
Omorenoniwara	Oh-moh-reh-nom-WAH-rah	Meant not to suffer	Benin	West Africa
Omorose	Oh-moh-ROH-seh	My beautiful child	Benin	West Africa
Omosede	Oh-MOH-seh-deh	A child counts more than a king	Benin	West Africa
Omosupe	Oh-MOH-soo-peh	A child is the most precious thing	Benin	West Africa
Oni	AW-nee	Born in a sacred abode	Yoruba	West Africa
Osayioniwabo	Oh-sah-yohm-WAH-boh	God will help us	Benin	West Africa

NIGERIA

Name	Pronounciation	Meaning	Origin	Region
Osemweoyenmwen	Ohsem-wo-yen-wen	Precious	Edo	West Africa
Oseye	Oh-SEH-yeh	Happy one	Benin	West Africa
Shade	Shah-DEH	Sweetly singing	Yoruba	West Africa
Shiminege	Shee-mee-NEH-geh	Let us perceive the future	Tiv	West Africa
Taiwo	TAH-ee-woh	First born of twins	Yoruba	West Africa
Titilayo	Tee-tee-lah-YOH	Eternal happiness	Yoruba	West Africa
Uchefuna	Oo-cheh-foo-NAH	I have my wits about me	Ibo	West Africa
Urbi	OOR-bee	Princess	Benin	West Africa
Yahimba	Yah-him-BAH	There is nothing like home	Tiv	West Africa
Yejide	Yeh-jee-DEH	The image of mother	Yoruba	West Africa
Yetunde	Yeh-TOON-deh	Mother returns	Yoruba	West Africa
Zuna	ZOO-nah	Abundance	Bobangi	West Africa

SOUTH AFRICA

Name	Pronunciation	Meaning	Origin	Region
Mafuane	Mah-FOO-ah-neh	Soil	Bachopi	South Africa
Mandisa	Man-DEE-sah	Sweet	Xhosa	South Africa
Nkosazana	N-koh-sah-ZAH-nah	Princess	Xhosa	South Africa
Nobanzi	Noh-BAN-zee	Width	Xhosa	South Africa
Nomalanga	Noh-mah-LANG-gah	Sunny	Zulu	South Africa
Nombeko	Nom-BEH-KOH	Respect	Xhosa	South Africa

SOUTH AFRICA

Name	Pronunciation	Meaning	Origin	Region
Nomble	NOM-bleh	Beauty	Xhosa	South Africa
Nomuula	Noh-MOO-lah	Rain	Xhosa	South Africa
Nonyameko	Nong-ya-MEH-koh	Patience	Xhosa	South Africa
Serafina	Seh-rah-FEE-nah	Burning passion	Xhosa	South Africa
Siboniso	See-boh-NEE-soh	A sign	Zulu	South Africa
Siphiwe	See-PEE-weh	We were given	Zulu	South Africa
Thandiwe	Tan-DEE-weh	Loving one	Xhosa	South Africa
Themba	TEHM-bah	Trusted	Zulu	South Africa

SUDAN

Name	Pronunciation	Meaning	Origin	Country	Region	Gender
Nyawela	Nyah-WEH-lah	On a journey	Shulla	Sudan	Central Africa	F
Nyimak	NYEE-mahk	Little fire	Shulla	Sudan	Central Africa	F
Nyirej	NYEE-rehj	Little fish	Shulla	Sudan	Central Africa	F

TANZANIA

Name	Pronunciation	Meaning	Origin	Region
Bupe	BOO-peh	Hospitality	Nyakyusa	East Africa
Doto	DOH-toh	Younger child of twins	Zaramo	East Africa
Kanoni	Kah-NOH-nee	Little bird	Ulaya	East Africa
Kizuwanda	Kee-zu-WAHN-dah	Last born child	Zaramo	East Africa

TANZANIA

Name	Pronunciation	Meaning	Origin	Region
Kuiwa	KOOL-wah	First of twins	Zaramo	East Africa
Kulwa	KOOL-wah	First of twins	Zaramo	East Africa
Kyalamboka	Kee-ah-lam-BOH-kah	God save me	Nyakyusa	East Africa
Mkegani	M-keh-GAH-nee	Child of disrespectful wife	Zaramo	East Africa
Mundufiki	Moon-doo-FEE-kee	Good for nothing	Nyakyusa	East Africa
Mwamuila	M-wah-moo-EE-lah	Bdrn during the war	Zaramo	East Africa
Mwanawa	Mwah-NAH-wah	First born of my children	Zaramo	East Africa
Mwanjaa	M-wah-nan-JAAH	Born during famine	Zaramo	East Africa
Ngabile	N-gah-BEE-leh	I have got it	Nyakyusa	East Africa
Sekelaga	Seh-keh-LAH-gah	Rejoice	Nyakyusa	East Africa
Sigolwide	See-gol-WEE-deh	My ways are straight	Nyakyusa	East Africa
Sikambagila	See-kam-bah-GHEE-lah	It doesn't suit him	Nyakyusa	East Africa
Suma	SOO-mah	Ask	Nyakyusa	East Africa
Syandene	See-ahn-DEH-neh	Punctual	Nyakyusa	East Africa
Tulimbwelu	Too-lim-BWEH-loo	We are in the light	Nyakyusa	East Africa
Tulinagwe	Too-lee-NAH-gweh	God is with us	Nyakyusa	East Africa
Tumpe	TOOM-peh	Let us thank God	Nyakyusa	East Africa
Tupokigwe	Too~poh~keegweh	We are safe	Nyakyusa	East Africa
Tusajigwe	Too-SAH-jee-gweh	We are blessed	Nyakyusa	East Africa
Tuwalole	Too-wah-loh-LEH	Exemplary	Zaramo	East Africa
Twaponilo	Too-ah-poh-nee-LOH	We are saved	Nyakyusa	East Africa

UGANDA

Name	Pronunciation	Meaning	Origin	Region
Abbo	AH-boh	A condiment	Mudama	East Africa
Emojung	EH-mo-yong	The old one	Karamojong	East Africa
Kissa	Kiss-SAH	Born after twins	Buganda	East Africa
Mangeni	Man-GHEH-nee	Fish	Musamia	East Africa
Masani	Mah-SAH-nee	Has a gap between the front teeth	Buganda	East Africa
Nabirye	Nah-beer-YEH	One who produces twins	Luganda	East Africa
Nabukwasi	Nah-boo-KWAH-see	Bad housekeeper	Luganda	East Africa
Nabulungi	Nah-boo-long-GHEE	Beautiful one	Buganda	East Africa
Nafuna	Nah-fro-NAH	Delivered feet first	Luganda	East Africa
Nalongo	Nah-long-GOH	Mother of twins	Buganda	East Africa
Namono	NAH-moh-noh	Younger of twins	Buganda	East Africa
Namusobiya	Nah-moo-so-beeah	One who has offended	Musoga	East Africa
Nasiche	Nah-SEE-cheh	Born in the locust season	Musoga	East Africa
Wesesa	Weh-seh-SAH	Careless	Musoga	East Africa
Zesiro	ZEH-see-roh	Elder of twins	Buganda	East Africa

ZIMBABWE

Name	Pronunciation	Meaning	Origin	Region
Chemwapuwa	Chem-WAH-poo-wah	That which you are given	Shona	South Africa
Chipo	CHEE-poh	Gift	Shona	South Africa
Japera	Jah-PEH-rah	We are finished	Shona	South Africa
Jendayi	Jen-DAH-yee	Give thanks	Shona	South Africa
Kambo	KAM-boh	Unlucky	Shona	South Africa
Maiba	MAH-ee-bah	Grave	Shona	South Africa
Mudiwa	Moo-DEE-wah	Beloved	Shona	South Africa
Muzwudzani	Mooz-woo-DZAH-nee	Whom should we tell	Shona	South Africa
Mwaurayeni	Mwah-O-rah-YEH-nee	What have you killed?	Shona	South Africa
Mwazwenyi	Mwaz-WEN-yee	What have you heard?	Shona	South Africa
Rufaro	Roo-FAH-roh	Happiness	Shona	South Africa
Sangeya	San-GEH-yah	Hate me	Shona	South Africa
Shoorai	Shoh-oh-RAH-ee	A broom that sweeps	Shona	South Africa
Sukutai	Soo-koo-TAH-ee	Squeeze	Shona	South Africa

AFRICAN MALE NAMES

BOTSWANA

Name	Pronunciation	Meaning	Origin	Region
Baruti	Bah-roo-tee	Teacher	Tswana	South Africa
Fenyang	Fehn-YANG	Conqueror	Tswana	South Africa
Goatsemodime	Khoat-seh-moh-dee-,neh	God knows	Tswana	South Africa
Kefentse	Keh-fent-seh	A conqueror	Tswana	South Africa
Kopano	Koh-pah-noh	Union	Tswana	South Africa
Letsego	Let-seh-goh	Arm	Tswana	South Africa
Montsho	Mohn-sho	Black	Tswana	South Africa
Mosegi	Moh-seh-ghee	Tailor	Tswana	South Africa
Moswen	Mohss-wehn	Light in color	Tswana	South Africa
Mothudi	Moh-too-dee	Smith	Tswana	South Africa
Tale	Tah-leh	Green	Tswana	South Africa
Tau	Tah-oo	Lion	Tswana	South Africa
Tebogo	Teh-boh-goh	We are grateful	Tswana	South Africa

ETHIOPIA

Name	Pronunciation	Meaning	Origin	Region
Girma	Gar-mah	Majesty	Amharic	North Africa

GHANA

Name	Pronunciation	Meaning	Origin	Region
Abeeku	AH-Bay-Koo	Born on wednesday	Fante	West Africa
Addae	Ah-DAH-Eh	Morning sun	Akan	West Africa
Adeben	Ah-Deh-BEHN	The twelfth born	Akan	West Africa

GHANA

Name	Pronunciation	Meaning	Origin	Region
Adika	Ah-Dee-KAH	First child of a second husband	Ewe	West Africa
Adofo	Ah-DOH-Foh	A courageous warrior	Akan	West Africa
Adom	Ah-DOHM	Help from god	Akan	West Africa
Agyei	Ahg-JAY-Ee	Messenger from god	Akan	West Africa
Agyeman	Ahg-YEH-Man	Fourteenth born	Akan	West Africa
Agymah	Ahg-Jee-MAH	One who leaves his community	Fante	West Africa
Akua	A-KOO-Ah	Born on thursday	Fante	West Africa
Akwetee	Ah-KWAY-Teh	Younger of twins	Ga	West Africa
Ametefe	Ah-MEH-Teh-Feh	Child born after father's death	Ewe	West Africa
Ampah	AHM-Pah	Trust	Akan	West Africa
Anane	Ah-NAH-Neh	The fourth son	Akan	West Africa
Ankoma	Ahn-KOH-Mah	Last born of parents	Akan	West Africa
Anum	AH-Noom	Fifth born	Akan	West Africa
Ata	AH-Ta	One of twins	Fante	West Africa
Atsu	At-SOO	Younger of twins	Ewe	West Africa
Atu	Ah-TOO	Born on saturday	Fante	West Africa
Awotwe	A-WOH-Tweh	Eighth born	Akan	West Africa
Badu	Bah-DOO	The tenth	Akan	West Africa
Coblah	Koh-BLAH	Born on tuesday	Ewe	West Africa
Coffie	Koh-FEE	Born on friday	Ewe	West Africa
Commie	KOH-Mee	Born on saturday	Ewe	West Africa
Coujoe	Koh-JOH	Born on monday	Ewe	West Africa
Donkor	Dohn-Koh	The humble one	Akan	West Africa
Ebo	Eh-BOH	Born on tuesday	Fante	West Africa
Fenuku	Fay-Noo-KOO	Born after term	Fante	West Africa
Fenuku	Feh-Noo-KOO	Born after twins	Fante	West Africa
Fifi	Fee-FEE	Born on friday	Fante	West Africa
Gyasi	JAH-See	Wonderful one	Akan	West Africa

GHANA

Name	Pronunciation	Meaning	Origin	Region
Jojo	Joh-JOH	Born on monday	Fante	West Africa
Kodwo	Koh-DWOH	Born on monday	Twi	West Africa
Kofi	Koh-FEE	Born on friday	Twi	West Africa
Kojo	Koh-JOH	Born on monday	Akan	West Africa
Kontar	KOHN-Tar	An only child	Akan	West Africa
Kpodo	Kh-Poh-DOH	The elder of twins	Ewe	West Africa
Kufuo	Koo-FOO-Oh	Father shared birth pangs	Fante	West Africa
Kwabena	KWAH-Beh-Nah	Born on tuesday	Akan	West Africa
Kwakou	Kwah-KOO	Born on wednesday	Ewe	West Africa
Kwame	KWAH-Meh	Born on saturday	Akan	West Africa
Kwasi	KWAH-See	Born on sunday	Akan	West Africa
Lumo	LOO-Moh	Born face downwards	Ewe	West Africa
Manu	Mah-NOO	The second born	Akan	West Africa
Mawulawde	Mah-Woo-Lah-Weh-DAY	God will provide	Ewe	West Africa
Mawuli	MAH-Woo-Lee	There is a god	Ewe	West Africa
Mensah	MEN-Sah	Third son	Ewe	West Africa
Minkah	MEEN-Kah	Justice	Akan	West Africa
Msrah	M-SRAH	Sixth born	Akan	West Africa
Msrah	M-SRAH	Sixth born	Akan	West Africa
Nkrumah	N-KROO-Mah	Ninth born	Akan	West Africa
Nsoah	N-Soh-AH	Seventh born	Akan	West Africa
Nyamekye	N-Yah-MEH-Kee-Eh	Gods gift	Akan	West Africa
Oko	Oh-KOH	Elder of twins	Ga	West Africa
Osei	Oh-SEH-Ee	Noble	Fante	West Africa
Quaashie	Kwah-SHEE	Born on sunday	Ewe	West Africa
Sisi	See-SEE	Born on a sunday	Fante	West Africa
Tse	Tseh	Younger of twins	Ewe	West Africa
Tuako	Twah-KOH	Eleventh born	Ga	West Africa

GHANA

Name	Pronunciation	Meaning	Origin	Region
Twia	TWEE-Ah	Born after twins	Fante	West Africa
Yafeu	Yah-FEH-Oh	Bold	Fante	West Africa
Yao	YAH-Oh	Born on thursday	Ewe	West Africa
Yawo	YAH-Woh	Born on a thursday	Akan	West Africa
Yoofi	Yoh-Oh-FEE	Born on friday	Akan	West Africa
Yooku	Yoh-Oh-KOO	Born on wednesday	Fante	West Africa
Yorkoo	Yor-KOO	Born on thursday	Fante	West Africa

KENYA

Name	Pronunciation	Meaning	Origin	Region
Chilemba	Chee-LEHM-bah	Turban	Mwera	East Africa
Chitundu	Chee-TOON-doo	Birds' nest	Mwera	East Africa
Chiumbo	Chee-oom-boh	A little creation	Mwera	East Africa
Gacoki	GAH-sho-key	One who returns	Kikuyu	East Africa
Gakere	Gah-KEH-reh	Muscular	Kikuyu	East Africa
Gakuru	GAH-koh-row	Elderly one	Kikuyu	East Africa
Gatete	GAH-teh-teh	A milk gourd	Kikuyu	East Africa
Gathee	GAH-the-eh	Elderly one	Kikuyu	East Africa
Gathii	GAH-thee-ee	A wanderer	Kikuyu	East Africa
Gatimu	GAH-tee-mo	A spear	Kikuyu	East Africa
Gethii	GEH-thee-ee	Wanderer	Kikuyu	East Africa
Gichinga	GEH-shee-gah	A firebrand	Kikuyu	East Africa
Gicicio	GEH-shee-shio	Mirror	Kikuyu	East Africa
Gikuyu	GEH-koh-yoh	Founder of the Agikuyu nation	Kikuyu	East Africa
Githinji	GEH-the-gee	A butcher	Kikuyu	East Africa
Gitonga	GEH-toh-gah	Wealthy one	Kikuyu	East Africa
Hiuhu	Hee-oh-HOO	He is hot	Kikuyu	East Africa

50

KENYA

Name	Pronunciation	Meaning	Origin	Region
Ikinya	EE-key-nyah	A single step	Kikuyu	East Africa
Iregi	EE-reh-ghee	A rebel	Kikuyu	East Africa
Irungu	EE-rohn-goh	Makes right, reformer	Kikuyu	East Africa
Ita	EE-tah	A war raid	Kikuyu	East Africa
Itimu	EE-tee-moh	A spear	Kikuyu	East Africa
Jaramogi	JAH-rah-moh-ghee	Courageous	Luo	East Africa
Jimiyu	JEE-mee-yoo	Born in the summer season	Abaluhya	East Africa
Jomo	JOH-moh	Burning spear	Kikuyu	East Africa
Kagai	KAH-gah-ee	The divider	Kikuyu	East Africa
Kagunda	KAH-gohn-dah	Of the land	Kikuyu	East Africa
Kahiga	KAH-hee-gah	A rock	Kikuyu	East Africa
Kairu	KAH-ee-roh	Black one	Kikuyu	East Africa
Kamau	Kah-MAH-oo	Quiet warrior	Kikuyu	East Africa
Kanja	KHAN-jah	From the outside	Kikuyu	East Africa
Kanoro	KHAN-oh-roo	Sharpens the sword	Kikuyu	East Africa
Karani	KAH-rah-nee	Aide, secretary	Kikuyu	East Africa
Karega	KAH-reh-gah	A rebel	Kikuyu	East Africa
Kariuki	KAH-ree-oh-kee	A child reincarnated	Kikuyu	East Africa
Kariuki	KAH-ree-okee	Born again	Kikuyu	East Africa
Kiambiroiro	Keh-am-bee-ROH-ee-roh	Mountain of blackness	Kikuyu	East Africa
Kianjahe	Keh-an-JAH-heh	Mountain of beans	Kikuyu	East Africa
Kiano	KEH-ah-noh	The wizards tools	Kikuyu	East Africa
Kianyandaarwa	Keh-ah-nee-yan-DAR-wah	Mountain of hides	Kikuyu	East Africa
Kiara	KEH-ah-rah	A finger	Kikuyu	East Africa

KENYA

Name	Pronunciation	Meaning	Origin	Region
Kihara	KEH-ha-rah	A bald patch	Kikuyu	East Africa
Kihiga	KEH-hee-gah	Rock	Kikuyu	East Africa
Kimathi	KEH-mah-thee	Kenyan freedom fighter	Kikuyu	East Africa
Kimotho	KEH-moh-tho	The left hand (left handed)	Kikuyu	East Africa
Kinoro	KEH-noh-roh	Sharpener of knives	Kikuyu	East Africa
Kinyua	KEHN-you-ah	One who drinks	Kikuyu	East Africa
Kioi	KEH-oh-ee	Bears heavy burdens	Kikuyu	East Africa
Kirimi	KEH-re-mee	A farmer	Kikuyu	East Africa
Kirinyaga	Keh-rehn-YAH-gah	Mountain of brightness (i.e. Mt. Kenya)	Kikuyu	East Africa
Kithingi	KEH-thee-gee	A butcher	Kikuyu	East Africa
Koigi	KOH-ee-gee	One who speaks	Kikuyu	East Africa
Kuguru	KOH-go-row	A leg	Kikuyu	East Africa
Lipapwiche	Lee-pap-WEE-chay	Torn	Mwera	East Africa
Macaria	MAH-shah-ree-ah	Seeker	Kikuyu	East Africa
Maina	MAH-ee-nah	A father of the Agikuyu nation	Kikuyu	East Africa
Maitho	MAH-ee-thoh	Eyes to see with	Kikuyu	East Africa
Makalani	Mah-kah-LAH-nee	Clerk, one skllled in writing	Mwera	East Africa
Makori	Mah-KOH-ree	Born on the way	Kisii	East Africa
Mathaathi	Mah-THAH-thee	Name of an age-group	Kikuyu	East Africa
Matu	MAH-two	The clouds	Kikuyu	East Africa
Maundu	MAH-oh-doh	This is a different thing	Kikuyu	East Africa

KENYA

Name	Pronunciation	Meaning	Origin	Region
Mawagali	Mah-wah-GAH-lee	Numerous	Abaluhya	East Africa
Mbogo	BOH-goh	The buffalo	Kikuyu	East Africa
Mbogo	BOH-goh	Buffalo	Kikuyu	East Africa
Mbui	BOO-ay	Grey hairs	Kikuyu	East Africa
Miano	MEH-ah-no	Wizards tools	Kikuyu	East Africa
Migwi	MEH-goo-ay	Arrows	Kikuyu	East Africa
Mokabi	Moh-kah-bee	Of the Maasai people	Kikuyu	East Africa
Morani	MOH-rah-nee	Warrior	Kisii	East Africa
Mpenda	M-PEHN-dah	Lover	Mwera	East Africa
Muga	MOO-gah	Confident of one truth	Kisii	East Africa
Mugendi	MOH-gehn-dee	Guests, passersby	Kikuyu	East Africa
Mugi	MOH-gheh	Wise one	Kikuyu	East Africa
Mugo	MOH-goh	Prophet	Kikuyu	East Africa
Muiru	MOH-ee-roh	Black one	Kikuyu	East Africa
Mukanda	MOH-kahn-dah	Strong cord	Kikuyu	East Africa
Mukhwana	Moo-KWAH-nah	Born as a twin	Abaluhya	East Africa
Mukiri	MOH-kee-ree	Silent one	Kikuyu	East Africa
Mukuru	Moh-koh-row	Elderly one	Kikuyu	East Africa
Munene	MOH-neh-neh	Big, great	Kikuyu	East Africa
Munoru	MOH-noh-roo	Fat one	Kikuyu	East Africa
Muraguri	MOH-rah-goh-ree	A seer	Kikuyu	East Africa
Murathi	MOH-rah-thee	A prophet	Kikuyu	East Africa
Muraya	MOH-rah-yah	Tall one	Kikuyu	East Africa
Muriithi	MOH-ray-thee	A shepard	Kikuyu	East Africa
Murimi	MOH-ray-mee	A farmer	Kikuyu	East Africa
Muriu	MOH-ree-oh	Son	Kikuyu	East Africa
Muriuki	MOH-ree-oh-key	One who is reborn	Kikuyu	East Africa

KENYA

Name	Pronunciation	Meaning	Origin	Region
Muroki	MOH-roh-kee	Comes with the dawn	Kikuyu	East Africa
Muruthi	MOH-row-thee	Lion	Kikuyu	East Africa
Mutahi	MOH-tah-hee	A raider	Kikuyu	East Africa
Mutegi	MOH-teh-gee	Hunter, trapper	Kikuyu	East Africa
Mutemi	MOH-teh-mee	King of the Agikuyu	Kikuyu	East Africa
Muthee	MOH-thee	An elder	Kikuyu	East Africa
Muthemba	MOH-them-bah	One of a kind	Kikuyu	East Africa
Muthengi	MOH-then-ghee	He move around	Kikuyu	East Africa
Mutheru	MOH-theh-roo	Cleansed	Kikuyu	East Africa
Muthomi	MOH-thoh-mee	A scholar	Kikuyu	East Africa
Muthuri	MOH-thuu-ree	An elder	Kikuyu	East Africa
Mutira	MOH-tee-rah	A counselor or advisor	Kikuyu	East Africa
Mutiri	MOH-tee-ree	A counselor or advisor	Kikuyu	East Africa
Mutitu	MOH-tee-toh	A forest	Kikuyu	East Africa
Mutonyi	MOH-ton-nyee	He enters	Kikuyu	East Africa
Mutua	MOH-too-ah	Reconciles differences	Kikuyu	East Africa
Muturi	MOH-too-ree	A craftsman	Kikuyu	East Africa
Muugi	MOH-oh-gay	Intelligent	Kikuyu	East Africa
Mwangi	Mwahn-gee	Seizes the nation, victorious	Kikuyu	East Africa
Mwara	MWAH-rah	Inteligent	Kikuyu	East Africa
Mwarania	MWAH-rah-nia	Brings together, negotiator	Kikuyu	East Africa
Mwaria	MWAH-ree-ah	One who speaks alot	Kikuyu	East Africa
Mwenda	MWEHN-duh	One who loves	Kikuyu	East Africa

KENYA

Name	Pronunciation	Meaning	Origin	Region
Nangila	NAN-ghee-lah	Born on a journey	Abaluhya	East Africa
Nangwaya	Nahn-GWAH-yah	Dont trifle with me	Mwera	East Africa
Ndegwa	DEHG-wah	A bull	Kikuyu	East Africa
Ndemi	DEH-mee	Founders of the Agikuyu nation	Kikuyu	East Africa
Nderu	DEH-roo	Bearded one	Kikuyu	East Africa
Ndwiga	DWEE-gah	A giraffe	Kikuyu	East Africa
Ngare	GAH-ray	A leopard	Kikuyu	East Africa
Ngigi	Gee-GAY	A grasshopper	Kikuyu	East Africa
Ngumo	GOO-moh	Fame	Kikuyu	East Africa
Njama	JAH-mah	A council e.g. War council.	Kikuyu	East Africa
Njata	JAH-tah	Star	Kikuyu	East Africa
Njau	JAH-oh	Strong calf	Kikuyu	East Africa
Njiraini	Jay-rah-ee-NAY	On the road	Kikuyu	East Africa
Njiru	Gee-ROH	Black one	Kikuyu	East Africa
Njogu	Joh-GOO	Elephant	Kikuyu	East Africa
Njora	Joh-RAH	A scabbard i.e. For a sword	Kikuyu	East Africa
Njowga	N-JOH-gah	Shoes	Mwera	East Africa
Njururi	JOE-roh-ree	Wanderer	Kikuyu	East Africa
Nyachae	NYAH-chah-ay	Generous	Kisii	East Africa
Nyaga	NYAH-gah	Brightness or Ostrich	Kikuyu	East Africa
Nyamu	NYAH-moh	Animal	Kikuyu	East Africa
Nyatui	N-YAH-too-ee	Fighter of leopards	Abaluhya	East Africa
Nyoike	NYOH-ee-keh	Stands alone	Kikuyu	East Africa
Obuya	OH-boo-yah	Born when the garden was overgrown	Luo	East Africa

KENYA

Name	Pronunciation	Meaning	Origin	Region
Ochieng	OH-chee-eng	Born at mid day	Luo	East Africa
Ochieng	OH-chee-eng	Born in the daytime	Luo	East Africa
Odikinyi	OH-dee-key-nyee	Born in the early morning	Luo	East Africa
Odongo	OH-dohn-goh	Second of twins	Luo	East Africa
Odour	OH-doo-oh-rr	Born after midnight	Luo	East Africa
Ohon	OH-hon	The name is preserved (after the death of an elder)	Luo	East Africa
Ojwang	OH-jwahn-g	Survived despite neglect	Luo	East Africa
Okello	OH-keh-loh	Born after twins	Luo	East Africa
Okeyo	OH-keh-yoh	Born during the harvest	Luo	East Africa
Okoth	OH-koh-th	Born during the rainy season	Luo	East Africa
Okoth	Oh-KOTH	Born when it was raining	Luo	East Africa
Oluoch	Oh-loo-OHCH	Born on a cloudy day	Luo	East Africa
Oluoch	OH-loo-oh-ch	Born on a overcast morning	Luo	East Africa
Omariba	OH-mah-ree-bah	Clay	Kisii	East Africa
Omondi	OH-mohn-dee	Born at dawn	Luo	East Africa
Omwancha	OHM-wahn-cha	He loves pepole	Kisii	East Africa
Ongweng	OHNG-when	Born during the time of white ants	Luo	East Africa
Onindo	OH-neen-doh	Mother slept alot during pregnancy	Luo	East Africa

KENYA

Name	Pronunciation	Meaning	Origin	Region
Onkwani	OHN-kwah-nee	He talks a lots	Kisii	East Africa
Onyango	OHN-yah-goh	Born about mid day	Luo	East Africa
Opiyo	OH-pee-oh	First of twins	Luo	East Africa
Osogo	OH-soh-goh	The Osogo bird attended the birth	Luo	East Africa
Othiamba	Oh-tee-ahm-BAH	Born in the afternoon	Luo	East Africa
Othiambo	OH-thee-ahm-boh	Born late in the evening	Luo	East Africa
Otieno	OH-tee-eh-no	Born at night	Luo	East Africa
Ouma	Oh-oo-AMH	Born through Caesarian surgery	Luo	East Africa
Owino	OH-wee-no	Born with the cord around them	Luo	East Africa
Owiti	OH-wee-tcc	Born after misfortune	Luo	East Africa
Owuor	OH-woh-rr	Born in the mid morning	Luo	East Africa
Riitho	Ree-THOH	An eye to see with	Kikuyu	East Africa
Ruguru	ROH-goh-row	Comes from the west	Kikuyu	East Africa
Ruhiu	ROH-hee-oh	Sword	Kikuyu	East Africa
Runo	ROO-noh	A fold	Kikuyu	East Africa
Sokoro	SOH-koh-roh	Named after grandfather	Kisii	East Africa
Thabiti	Thah-BEE-tee	A true man	Mwera	East Africa
Tuwile	Too-WEE-leh	Death is inevitable	Mwera	East Africa
Waga	WAH-gah	The eldest died	Luo	East Africa
Waithaka	WAH-ee-thah-kah	Of the land	Kikuyu	East Africa

KENYA

Name	Pronunciation	Meaning	Origin	Region
Waitimu	WAH-ee-tee-moh	Born of the spear	Kikuyu	East Africa
Waiyaki	WAI-yah-kee	A great leader of the Agikuyu	Kikuyu	East Africa
Waiyaki	WAH-ee-yah-kee	Famous leader of the Agikuyu	Kikuyu	East Africa
Wamai	WAH-mah-ee	Come from the water	Kikuyu	East Africa
Wamugunda	WAH-moh-gohn-dah	Of the land	Kikuyu	East Africa
Wamukota	WAH-moo-koh-tah	Left-handed	Abaluhya	East Africa
Wamwara	WAHM-wah-rah	Intelligent	Kikuyu	East Africa
Wangombe	WAHN-goh-beh	Of the cattle	Kikuyu	East Africa
Wangondu	WAHN-goh-doo	Of the sheep	Kikuyu	East Africa
Wanyanga	WAHN-yahn-gah	The name is preserved (after death of an elder)	Luo	East Africa
Waruhiu	WAH-roh-hee-oh	Bears a weapon always	Kikuyu	East Africa
Warui	WAH-roh-ay	Come from the river	Kikuyu	East Africa
Waweru	WAH-we-roh	Born of the plains	Kikuyu	East Africa

KENYA-TANZANIA

Name	Pronunciation	Meaning	Origin	Region
Abasi	Ah-BAH-see	Stern	Swahili	East Africa
Abdalla	Ab-DAHL-lah	Servant of God	Swahili	East Africa
Abdu	Ab-DOO	Worshipper of God	Swahili	East Africa
Abdul	Ab-DOOL	Servant of the lord	Swahili	East Africa
Abedi	A-BEH-dee	Worshiper	Swahili	East Africa
Abubakar	Ah-BOO-bah-kar	Noble	Swahili	East Africa
Abuu	Ah-BOO	Father	Swahili	East Africa
Adam	A-DAM	First human being	Swahili	East Africa
Adamu	A-DAM-ooh	Adam	Swahili	East Africa
Adili	Ah-DEE-lee	Just	Swahili	East Africa
Adnan	Ahd-NAN	Good fortune	Swahili	East Africa
Ahmed	Ah-MED	One who is praise worthy	Swahili	East Africa
Ainran	Aeen-RAHN	Prosperity	Swahili	East Africa
Akbar	AHK-bah	Greater	Swahili	East Africa
Akida	A-kee-DAH	Belief	Swahili	East Africa
Akili	Ah-KEE-lee	Intelligent	Swahili	East Africa
Akram	Ah-CRAM	More generous	Swahili	East Africa
Alamini	Ah-LAH-mee-nee	Trustworthy	Swahili	East Africa
Alhaadi	Al-had-ee	Guide	Swahili	East Africa
Ali	Ah-LEE	Exalted	Swahili	East Africa
Amaad	Ah-mad	Support	Swahili	East Africa
Amani	Ah-MAH-nee	Peace	Swahili	East Africa
Amar	Ah-MAH	Long life	Swahili	East Africa
Ambar	AHM-bah	Ambergris	Swahili	East Africa
Ame	Ah-MEH	Universal	Swahili	East Africa
Amini	AH-mee-nee	Trustworthy	Swahili	East Africa
Amiri	AH-mee-ree	Prince	Swahili	East Africa
Anasa	AH-nah-sah	Entertainment	Swahili	East Africa
Antar	An-TAH	Hero	Swahili	East Africa

KENYA-TANZANIA

Name	Pronunciation	Meaning	Origin	Region
Anwar	An-WAH	Bright	Swahili	East Africa
Arif	AH-reef	Knowledgeable	Swahili	East Africa
Asad	Ah-SAHD	Lion	Swahili	East Africa
Asani	Ah-SAH-nee	Rebellious	Swahili	East Africa
Asante	AH-sahn-teh	You have been good, thank you	Swahili	East Africa
Ashur	Ah-SHOOR	Born during Islamic month Ashur	Swahili	East Africa
Athumani	AH-thuu-mah-nee	Third Khalifa	Swahili	East Africa
Atif	AH-teef	Compassionate	Swahili	East Africa
Ayubu	AH-yoo-boo	Perseverance	Swahili	East Africa
Azaan	Ah-zahn	Strength	Swahili	East Africa
Aziz	AH-zeez	Precious	Swahili	East Africa
Azizi	Ah-ZEE-zee	Precious	Swahili	East Africa
Baakir	BAH-keyr	The eldest	Swahili	East Africa
Baba	Bah-bah	Father	Swahili	East Africa
Babechi	Bah-BEH-chee	Father of Echi	Swahili	East Africa
Babu	BAH-buh	Grandfather	Swahili	East Africa
Badawi	BAH-duh-wee	Nomad	Swahili	East Africa
Badilini	BAH-dee-lee-nee	Change	Swahili	East Africa
Badrani	BAD-rah-nee	Full moon	Swahili	East Africa
Badru	BAH-droo	Born at the full moon	Swahili	East Africa
Baha	BAH-hah	Brilliance	Swahili	East Africa
Baka	BAH-kah	Permanence	Swahili	East Africa
Bakari	Bah-KAH-ree	One with great promise	Swahili	East Africa
Baraka	BAH-rah-kah	Blessings	Swahili	East Africa
Bashiri	BAH-she-ree	Predictor	Swahili	East Africa
Bausi	BAH-ooh-see	He sharpens (knives)	Swahili	East Africa
Bavual	BAH-vuh-ahl	Fisherman	Swahili	East Africa

KENYA-TANZANIA

Name	Pronunciation	Meaning	Origin	Region
Bilaal	Bee-LAHL	Calls to prayer	Swahili	East Africa
Bilali	Bee-LAH-lee	Calls to prayer	Swahili	East Africa
Boma	BOH-mah	Fortress	Swahili	East Africa
Boraafya	BOH-rah-ah-fear	Better health	Swahili	East Africa
Burhani	BOOH-ani	Proof	Swahili	East Africa
Bushiri	BOOH-she-ree	Predictor	Swahili	East Africa
Chacha	Cha-chah	Strong	Swahili	East Africa
Chaga	CHA-gar	Holiday	Swahili	East Africa
Chandu	CHAN-doo	Octopus	Swahili	East Africa
Chega	CHE-gah	Holiday	Swahili	East Africa
Cheja	CHE-jar	Holiday	Swahili	East Africa
Chimalsi	CHEE-mahl-see	Young and proud	Swahili	East Africa
Dada	DAH-da	Elder one	Swahili	East Africa
Dahoma	DAH-ho-mah	Long life	Swahili	East Africa
Dajan	DAH-jahn	Dark sky during a heavy rain	Swahili	East Africa
Daktari	DAHK-tah-ree	Doctor, healer	Swahili	East Africa
Damu	DAH-moo	Blood	Swahili	East Africa
Daraja	DAH-rah-jah	Bridge, stage	Swahili	East Africa
Darweshi	Dahr-WEH-shee	Holy one	Swahili	East Africa
Dau	DAH-ooh	Abbreviation of Daudi	Swahili	East Africa
Daud	DAH-oohd	David	Swahili	East Africa
Daudi	Dah-OO-dee	Beloved	Swahili	East Africa
Dhoruba	THOR-roo-BAH	Storm	Swahili	East Africa
Dini	DEE-nee	Faith, religion	Swahili	East Africa
Dogo	Doh-GOH	Small	Swahili	East Africa
Dumisha	Doo-mee-SHAH	Intimate friendship	Swahili	East Africa
Ekevu	EH-KEH-voo	Intelligent, enlightened	Swahili	East Africa
Elewa	EH-leh-wah	Very intelligent	Swahili	East Africa
Elimu	EH-lee-moo	Knowledge	Swahili	East Africa

KENYA-TANZANIA

Name	Pronunciation	Meaning	Origin	Region
Erevu	EH-reh-voo	Clever, talented	Swahili	East Africa
Fadhili	FAH-dee-lee	Virtuous	Swahili	East Africa
Fahim	FAH-him	Learned	Swahili	East Africa
Fakhri	FAHK-ree	Glory, honor	Swahili	East Africa
Faki	FAH-kee	Hollowr,	Swahili	East Africa
Fakihi	FAH-kee-hee	Wise	Swahili	East Africa
Faqihi	FAH-kee-hee	Wise	Swahili	East Africa
Faraji	Fah-RAH-jee	Consolation	Swahili	East Africa
Farhani	FAH-hah-nee	Happy	Swahili	East Africa
Farid	FAH-read	Unique	Swahili	East Africa
Faruki	FAH-roo-kee	Judicious	Swahili	East Africa
Fathi	FAH-thee	Victorious	Swahili	East Africa
Fauzi	FAH-ooh-zee	Successful	Swahili	East Africa
Fehed	FEH-hehd	Lynx, panther	Swahili	East Africa
Feisal	FEH-ee-sahl	Arbitrator	Swahili	East Africa
Feruzi	FEH-roo-zee	Turquoise	Swahili	East Africa
Fidel	Fee-DEHL	Faithful	Swahili	East Africa
Fikirini	Fee-KEY-ree-nee	Reflect	Swahili	East Africa
Fogo	FOH-goh	High	Swahili	East Africa
Fuad	FUH-ad	Heart	Swahili	East Africa
Fumo	FUH-moh	Majesty	Swahili	East Africa
Fumu	FUH-moo	Majesty	Swahili	East Africa
Fundikira	FUHN-dee-kee-rah	Learned	Swahili	East Africa
Funga	FUHN-gah	Tie, bind	Swahili	East Africa
Furaha	FUH-rah-ha	Happiness	Swahili	East Africa
Ghalib	GAH-leeb	Winner	Swahili	East Africa
Ghaniy	GAH-nee	Rich	Swahili	East Africa
Gharib	GAH-rib	Stranger, visitor	Swahili	East Africa
Gheilani	GEH-ee-lah-nee	Tropical tree	Swahili	East Africa
Ghofiri	GOH-fee-ree	Forgiveness, pardon	Swahili	East Africa
Haamid	HAH-mead	Grateful	Swahili	East Africa

KENYA-TANZANIA

Name	Pronunciation	Meaning	Origin	Region
Habib	Hah-BEEB	Beloved	Swahili	East Africa
Habibu	HAH-beeb-ooh	Beloved	Swahili	East Africa
Hafidh	HAH-feed	Preserver	Swahili	East Africa
Hafiz	HAH-fizz	Guardian	Swahili	East Africa
Haidar	HAH-ee-dah	Strong, stout	Swahili	East Africa
Hainidi	Hah-MEE-dee	Commendable	Swahili	East Africa
Haji	HAH-jee	Born during the month of pilgrimage to Mecca	Swahili	East Africa
Haki	HAH-kee	Right, justice	Swahili	East Africa
Hakim	HAH-keem	Judge	Swahili	East Africa
Hali	HAH-lee	Condition., state	Swahili	East Africa
Hamadi	Hah-MAH-dee	One who is praised	Swahili	East Africa
Hamdaan	HAM-dan	Praise	Swahili	East Africa
Hami	HAH-mee	Defend	Swahili	East Africa
Hamidi	Hah-MEE-dee	One to be commended	Swahili	East Africa
Hamisi	Hah-MEE-see	Born on Thursday	Swahili	East Africa
Hamza	HAH-mm-zah	Strong	Swahili	East Africa
Haoniyao	Hah-oh-nee-YAH-oh	Born at the time of a quarrel	Swahili	East Africa
Harambee	HAH-rahm-bay	Let's pull together	Swahili	East Africa
Harun	Hah-ROON	Messenger, Aharon, Aaron	Swahili	East Africa
Hasan	HAH-sahn	Good	Swahili	East Africa
Hasani	Hah-SAH-nee	Handsome	Swahili	East Africa
Hashil	HAH-sheel	Emigrant	Swahili	East Africa
Hashim	HAH-sheem	Honor	Swahili	East Africa
Hasnuu	HAS-noo	Handsome	Swahili	East Africa
Hatari	HAH-tah-ree	Danger	Swahili	East Africa
Hauli	HAH-oo-lee	Power, strength	Swahili	East Africa

KENYA-TANZANIA

Name	Pronunciation	Meaning	Origin	Region
Hekima	HEH-kee-MAH	Clever, wise	Swahili	East Africa
Heri	HEH-ree	Goodness	Swahili	East Africa
Heshima	HEH-shee-MAH	Highly esteemed	Swahili	East Africa
Heshimu	HEH-shee-moo	Honor, respect	Swahili	East Africa
Hilali	HEE-lah-lee	Crescent	Swahili	East Africa
Himidi	HEE-mee-dee	Grateful	Swahili	East Africa
Hisham	HEE-shaam	Generous	Swahili	East Africa
Hodari	HOH-duh-ree	Energetic, capable	Swahili	East Africa
Humud	HUH-muhd	Gracious	Swahili	East Africa
Hurani	HUH-rah-nee	Restive	Swahili	East Africa
Husani	Hoo-SAH-nee	Handsome	Swahili	East Africa
Huseni	HOO-seh-nee	Good	Swahili	East Africa
Husni	HOHS-nee	Goodness	Swahili	East Africa
Ibada	EE-bah-dah	Adoration	Swahili	East Africa
Idi	EE-dee	Born during the festival of Idd	Swahili	East Africa
Idriis	EE-drees	Prophet, he studies	Swahili	East Africa
Imaan	EE-man	Faith	Swahili	East Africa
Imamu	EE-mah-moo	Minister, preacher	Swahili	East Africa
Iman	EE-man	Faith	Swahili	East Africa
Imara	EE-mah-rah	Stamina, strength	Swahili	East Africa
Imarika	EE-mah-ree-kah	Be steadfast	Swahili	East Africa
Isa	EE-sah	Jesus	Swahili	East Africa
Isaam	EE-sam	Guard	Swahili	East Africa
Isilahi	EE-see-lah-hee	Reconciliation	Swahili	East Africa
Isimo	EE-see-mo	Quality	Swahili	East Africa
Isiyoshindika	EE-see-yoh-sheen-dee-kah	Unconquerable	Swahili	East Africa
Islam	EE-slam	Submission to God	Swahili	East Africa
Ismael	EE-smah-el	Prophet, he hears	Swahili	East Africa

KENYA-TANZANIA

Name	Pronunciation	Meaning	Origin	Region
Ismaili	EES-mah-ee-lee	Ishmael, he hears	Swahili	East Africa
Issa	Ee-SAH	God is our salvation	Swahili	East Africa
Jaafar	JAA-faar	Small river	Swahili	East Africa
Jabali	JAH-bah-lee	Strong as a rock	Swahili	East Africa
Jabari	Jah-BAH-ree	Courageous	Swahili	East Africa
Jabir	JAH-BEE-rr	Restorer	Swahili	East Africa
Jabiri	JAH-bee-ree	Comforter	Swahili	East Africa
Jafari	Jah-FAH-ree	Creek	Swahili	East Africa
Jaha	JAH-ha	Dignified	Swahili	East Africa
Jahi	JAH-hee	Dignity	Swahili	East Africa
Jahina	JAH-hee-nah	Brave, courageous	Swahili	East Africa
Jalali	JAH-lah-lee	Almighty	Swahili	East Africa
Jalil	JAH-leel	Exalted, honorable	Swahili	East Africa
Jalili	JAH-lee-lee	Exalted, dignified	Swahili	East Africa
Jamal	JAH-mahl	Elegance	Swahili	East Africa
Jamali	JAH-mah-lee	Beauty	Swahili	East Africa
Jamil	JAH-meel	Handsome	Swahili	East Africa
jasiri	JAH-see-ree	Fearless	Swahili	East Africa
Jauhar	JAH-oo-ha	Jewel, gem	Swahili	East Africa
Jawaad	JAH-wahd	Generous	Swahili	East Africa
Jecha	JEH-cha	Sunrise	Swahili	East Africa
Jefar	JEH-fah	Recovery	Swahili	East Africa
Jela	JEH-lah	Father in prison at birth	Swahili	East Africa
Jelani	Jeh-LAH-nee	Mighty one	Swahili	East Africa
Jemadari	JEH-mah-dah-ree	Army general	Swahili	East Africa
Jenebi	JEH-neh-bee	Affectionate	Swahili	East Africa
Jengo	JEHN-goh	Building, strength	Swahili	East Africa
jitu	JEE-too	Giant	Swahili	East Africa
Jitujeusi	JEE-too-jeh-oo-see	A black giant	Swahili	East Africa
Juma	JOO-mah	Born on Friday	Swahili	East Africa

KENYA-TANZANIA

Name	Pronunciation	Meaning	Origin	Region
Jumaane	Joo-MAH-neh	Born on Tuesday	Swahili	East Africa
Jumanne	Juh-MAHN-neh	Born on Tuesday	Swahili	East Africa
Jumba	JUHM-bah	Large building	Swahili	East Africa
jumbe	JUHM-beh	An important personage	Swahili	East Africa
Juta	Joo-TAH	Regret	Swahili	East Africa
Kabaila	KAH-bah-ee-lah	Person of high social status	Swahili	East Africa
Kabona	KAH-boh-nah	Priest	Swahili	East Africa
Kadhi	KAH-thee	Judge, wise person	Swahili	East Africa
Kadiri	KAH-dee-ree	Capable	Swahili	East Africa
Kafara	KAH-fah-rah	Sacrifice	Swahili	East Africa
Kafil	KAH-feel	Protector, responsible	Swahili	East Africa
Kahini	KAH-hee-nee	Priest, holy person	Swahili	East Africa
Kalamka	KAH-lahm-kah	Intelligent, well-informed	Swahili	East Africa
Kame	KAH-meh	Desolate	Swahili	East Africa
Kamil	KAH-meel	Perfect	Swahili	East Africa
Kamili	KAH-mah-lee	Perfection	Swahili	East Africa
Kanaifu	KAH-nah-ee-foo	A self-sufficient person	Swahili	East Africa
Kandoro	KAHN-doh-roh	A type of sweet potato	Swahili	East Africa
Kani	KAH-nee	Strength, energy	Swahili	East Africa
Karama	KAH-rah-mah	Generosity	Swahili	East Africa
Kareem	KAH-reem	Generous	Swahili	East Africa
Karim	KAH-reem	Generous	Swahili	East Africa
Karume	Kah-rooh-MEH	Master	Swahili	East Africa
Kasim	KAH-seem	Just	Swahili	East Africa
Kasisi	KAH-see-see	Priest, minister	Swahili	East Africa
Kesi	KEH-see	Judging, rational	Swahili	East Africa

KENYA-TANZANIA

Name	Pronunciation	Meaning	Origin	Region
Keto	KEH-toh	Depth	Swahili	East Africa
Khalafu	HAH-lah-foo	Succeed	Swahili	East Africa
Khalfan	Kahl-FAN	Successor	Swahili	East Africa
Khalfani	Kahl-FAH-nee	Destined to rule	Swahili	East Africa
Khalifa	KAH-lee-fah	Successor, viceroy	Swahili	East Africa
Khalil	KAH-leel	Sincere friend	Swahili	East Africa
Khamisi	Kah-MEE-see	Born on Thursday	Swahili	East Africa
Khatibu	KAH-tee-boo	Orator	Swahili	East Africa
Khelefu	HEH-leh-foo	Succeed	Swahili	East Africa
Kheri	HEH-ree	Goodness	Swahili	East Africa
Khiari	HEE-ah-ree	Preference	Swahili	East Africa
Kiango	Kee-an-GOH	Lampstand, light	Swahili	East Africa
Kibasila	KEE-bah-see-lah	Insight	Swahili	East Africa
Kibasira	KEE-bah-see-rah	Insight	Swahili	East Africa
Kibwana	KEE-bwah-nah	Young gentleman	Swahili	East Africa
Kibwe	KEE-bwoh	Blessed	Swahili	East Africa
Kifimbo	KEE-feem-boh	Stick	Swahili	East Africa
Kigoma .	KEE-goh-mah	Small drum, joy	Swahili	East Africa
Kijana	KEE-jah-nah	Youthful, young	Swahili	East Africa
Kijani	KEE-jah-nee	Warrior	Swahili	East Africa
Kimameta	KEE-mah-meh-tah	Diamond mine	Swahili	East Africa
Kimweri	KEEM-weh-ree	Ruler, chief	Swahili	East Africa
Kimya	KEEM-yah	Calm,quiet	Swahili	East Africa
Kinda	Keen-DAH	Young bird, chick, young and beautiful,	Swahili	East Africa
Kinjeketile	Keen-JEH-keh-tee-leh	He killed himself	Swahili	East Africa
Kinjikitile	Keen-JEE-kee-tee-leh	He killed himself	Swahili	East Africa
Kiongozi	KEE-on-goh-zee	Leader	Swahili	East Africa
Kipanga	KEE-pahn-gah	Falcon	Swahili	East Africa

KENYA-TANZANIA

Name	Pronunciation	Meaning	Origin	Region
Kisasi	KEE-sah-see	Revenge	Swahili	East Africa
Kitunda	KEE-tuhn-DAH	Small fruit	Swahili	East Africa
Kitunzi	KEE-tun-zee	Reward	Swahili	East Africa
Kitwana	Kee-TWAH-nah	Pledged to live	Swahili	East Africa
Kiume	KEE-ooh-meh	Masculine and strong	Swahili	East Africa
Kombo	KOH-m-boh	Impoverished, bent	Swahili	East Africa
Komboa	KOH-m-boh-ah	Redeemed, redemption	Swahili	East Africa
Kondo	KON-doh	War	Swahili	East Africa
Kongoresi	KOHN-goh-rez-ee	Old contest	Swahili	East Africa
Kristo	KH-ree-sto	Christian	Swahili	East Africa
Kudumu	KUH-duh-muh	Persevering, lasting	Swahili	East Africa
Kumbufu	KUH-m-buh-fuh	Person with excellent memory	Swahili	East Africa
Kumbuka	KUH-m-buh-kah	Person with excellent memory	Swahili	East Africa
Kunjufu	KUHN-juh-fuh	Cheerful and friendly	Swahili	East Africa
Kutisha	KUH-tee-shah	Tough, formidable	Swahili	East Africa
Kuumba	KUH-uh-mbah	Create, creativity	Swahili	East Africa
Kuweza	KUH-weh-zah	Very capable	Swahili	East Africa
Kwagalana	KWA-gah-lah-nah	Brotherly love	Swahili	East Africa
Kwanza	KWAN-zah	Beginning	Swahili	East Africa
Kweli	KWEH-lee	Honesty, truth	Swahili	East Africa
Lali	LAH-lee	Flexible	Swahili	East Africa
Latif	LAH-teef	Gentle	Swahili	East Africa
Liyongo	LEE-yohn-goh	Talks much	Swahili	East Africa
Lumumba	LUH-muhm-bah	Gifted	Swahili	East Africa
Maabade	MAA-bah-deh	Sanctuary	Swahili	East Africa
Maalik	MAA-lick	Experience	Swahili	East Africa

68

KENYA-TANZANIA

Name	Pronunciation	Meaning	Origin	Region
Maamuni	MAA-muh-nee	Blessed	Swahili	East Africa
Maarifa	MAA-ree-fah	Knowledge, skill	Swahili	East Africa
Mabruke	MAH-brew-keh	Blessed	Swahili	East Africa
Machano	MAH-cha-noh	Born on Wednesday	Swahili	East Africa
Machungwa	Mah-chew-ng-wah	Oranges	Swahili	East Africa
Machupa	Mah-CHOO-pah	Likes to drink	Swahili	East Africa
Madhubuti	MAH-DOO-buh-tee	Firm, steady	Swahili	East Africa
Magoma	Mah-goh-MAH	Celebration	Swahili	East Africa
Mahbub	MAH-boob	Beloved	Swahili	East Africa
Mahdi	MAH-dee	Rightfully guided	Swahili	East Africa
Mahfudh	MAH-food	Preserved	Swahili	East Africa
Mahiri	MAH-hee-ree	Skillful, clever	Swahili	East Africa
Mahmud	MAH-mood	Praised	Swahili	East Africa
Majaliwa	Mah-jah-lee-wah	By God's grace	Swahili	East Africa
Majid	Mah-jeed	Innovator	Swahili	East Africa
Majuto	Mah-juh-toh	Regret	Swahili	East Africa
Makame	MAH-kah-meh	High rank, ruler	Swahili	East Africa
Makamu	MAH-kah-muh	Dignified	Swahili	East Africa
Makini	MAH-kee-nee	Of good character	Swahili	East Africa
Makungu	MAH-kuhn-guh	Initiation	Swahili	East Africa
Makwetu	Mah-KWEH-too	Our place	Swahili	East Africa
Maliik	MAH-lick	King, owner	Swahili	East Africa
Malik	MAH-lick	King	Swahili	East Africa
Maliki	MAH-lick-ee	King, owner	Swahili	East Africa
Mambo	MAHM-boh	Matters, events	Swahili	East Africa
Manani	MAH-nah-nee	Almighty	Swahili	East Africa
Mandara	MAHN-dah-rah	Leader	Swahili	East Africa
Maneno	MAH-neh-noh	Words	Swahili	East Africa
Manzi	MAHN-zee	Residence	Swahili	East Africa
Manzili	MAHN-zee-lee	Sent by God	Swahili	East Africa

KENYA-TANZANIA

Name	Pronunciation	Meaning	Origin	Region
Mapute	Mah-puh-TEH	Empty, taken away	Swahili	East Africa
Marzuku	MAR-zoo-kuh	Blessed	Swahili	East Africa
Masamaha	MAH-sah-mah-hah	Forgiveness	Swahili	East Africa
Mashal	MAH-shahl	Torch	Swahili	East Africa
Mashuhuri	MAH-shoo-hoo-ree	Fame	Swahili	East Africa
Masilahi	MAH-see-lah-hee	Neccessity	Swahili	East Africa
Maskini	Mah-SKEE-nee	Poor	Swahili	East Africa
Masud	Mah-SOOD	Fortunate	Swahili	East Africa
Matari	Mah-TAH-ree	Rainy season	Swahili	East Africa
Matojo	Mah-TOH-joh	Markings on the face	Swahili	East Africa
Matwa	MAHT-wah	Sensible	Swahili	East Africa
Maulana	MAH-oo-lah-nah	Our master	Swahili	East Africa
Maulidi	Mah-oo-LEE-dee	Born during the month of Maulidi	Swahili	East Africa
Mbaarak	Mm-BAH-rahk	Blessed	Swahili	East Africa
Mbamba	BAHM-bah	Branch of a tree	Swahili	East Africa
Mbaruku	BAH-roo-koo	Blessed	Swahili	East Africa
Mbaya	BAH-ya	Bad, ugly	Swahili	East Africa
Mbingu	Been-GHU	Heaven	Swahili	East Africa
Mbishiri	BEE-shee-ree	Prophet	Swahili	East Africa
Mbita	M-BEE-tah	Born on a cold night	Swahili	East Africa
Mbwana	M-BWAH-nah	Master	Swahili	East Africa
Mchawi	Mm-CHA-wee	Magician	Swahili	East Africa
Mcheshi	Mm-CHE-shee	Very friendly	Swahili	East Africa
Mdahoma	Mm-DAH-hoh-mah	Long life	Swahili	East Africa
Mdogo	Mm-DOH-goh	Young	Swahili	East Africa
Mfaki	Mm-FAH-kee	Exalted	Swahili	East Africa
Mfalme	Mm-fahl-MEH	King	Swahili	East Africa
Mgeni	Mm-geh-nee	Visitor	Swahili	East Africa
Mhina	M-HEE-nah	Delightful	Swahili	East Africa

KENYA-TANZANIA

Name	Pronunciation	Meaning	Origin	Region
Milina	M-HEE-nah	Delightful	Swahili	East Africa
Mirza	MEER-zah	Prince	Swahili	East Africa
Miujiza	MEE-oo-jee-zah	Miracles	Swahili	East Africa
Mjibu	Mm-jee-boo	A nice person	Swahili	East Africa
Mjima	Mm-jee-mah	A helpful person	Swahili	East Africa
Mkadam	Mm-kah-dahm	Ahead	Swahili	East Africa
Mkamba	Mm-kahm-bah	A rope maker	Swahili	East Africa
Mkristo	Mm-KREE-stoh	A Christian	Swahili	East Africa
Mkubwa	M-KUH-bwah	Senior, great	Swahili	East Africa
Mkufunzi	M-KUH-fuhn-zee	Teacher	Swahili	East Africa
Mkwasi	Mm-KWAH-see	A wealthy person	Swahili	East Africa
Mosi	MOH-see	First born	Swahili	East Africa
Mrehe	Mm-REH-heh	Easy life	Swahili	East Africa
Mrekhe	Mm-REH-heh	Easy life	Swahili	East Africa
Msamaki	M-sah-MAH-kee	Like a fish	Swahili	East Africa
Msanaa	Mm-SAH-naa	A skillful man	Swahili	East Africa
Msemaji	Mm-SEH-mah-jee	Orator	Swahili	East Africa
Mshabaha	Mm-sha-bah-hah	Resemblance	Swahili	East Africa
Mshangama	Mm-SHAHN-gah-mah	Rising	Swahili	East Africa
Mshindi	Mm-SHEEN-dee	Victor, winner	Swahili	East Africa
Mtaalamu	Mm-tah-lah-MUH	Intellectual and scholarly	Swahili	East Africa
Mtafiti	Mm-TAH-fee-tee	Knowledge seeker	Swahili	East Africa
Mtangulizi	Mmtahn-guh-lee-zee	Leader, pioneer	Swahili	East Africa
Mtavila	Mm-tah-vee-lah	You'll eat it	Swahili	East Africa
Mtawa	Mm-tah-WAH	Devout person	Swahili	East Africa
Mtembei	MM-tehm-BEH-EE	One who roams about, a playboy	Swahili	East Africa
Mteremeshi	MM-teh-REHM-shee	Genial and friendly	Swahili	East Africa

71

KENYA-TANZANIA

Name	Pronunciation	Meaning	Origin	Region
Mteremo	Mm-TEH-reh-mo	Cheerful person	Swahili	East Africa
Mteule	Mm-TEH-oo-LEH	The chosen one	Swahili	East Africa
Mtoro	Mm-TOH-roh	A runaway	Swahili	East Africa
Mtoto	Mm-TOH-toh	Youngster, little boy	Swahili	East Africa
Mtulivu	Mm-TUH-lee-vuh	Quiet person	Swahili	East Africa
Mtume	Mm-TOO-meh	An apostle	Swahili	East Africa
Mtumwa	M-TOOM-wah	Pledged	Swahili	East Africa
Mubaadar	MUH-bah-dah	Undertakes	Swahili	East Africa
Mudrik	MUHD-reek	Intelligent, reasonable	Swahili	East Africa
Mufid	MUH-feed	Beneficial	Swahili	East Africa
Muhamadi	MUH-hah-mah-dee	Praised, commendable	Swahili	East Africa
Muhammad	Moo-HAH-mahd	Praised	Swahili	East Africa
Muhammed	MUH-hah-med	Praised, commendable	Swahili	East Africa
Muhashaham	MUH-hah-sha-hahm	Respected	Swahili	East Africa
Muhashmy	MUH-hah-shee-mee	Weak	Swahili	East Africa
Muhidini	MUH-hee-dee-nee	Revivalist	Swahili	East Africa
Muhsin	MUH-seen	Beneficent	Swahili	East Africa
Muhyiddin	MUH-yee-deen	Bestower of religion	Swahili	East Africa
Mukhtaar	MUHK-tah	Chosen	Swahili	East Africa
Mundhir	MUHN-deer	Sign, reminder	Swahili	East Africa
Mungu	MUHN-guh	God, fate, destiny	Swahili	East Africa
Munim	MUH-neem	Benefactor	Swahili	East Africa
Munir	MUH-near	Shining	Swahili	East Africa
Muombwa	MOO-om-boo-ah	Beseeched	Swahili	East Africa
Murtada	MOO-tah-dah	Disciplined	Swahili	East Africa
Musa	MOO-sah	Moses	Swahili	East Africa
Mustafa	MOOS-tah-far	Chosen one, Prophet	Swahili	East Africa

KENYA-TANZANIA

Name	Pronunciation	Meaning	Origin	Region
Muumin	MOO-meen	Believer	Swahili	East Africa
Muyaka	MOO-yah-kah	Good and truthful	Swahili	East Africa
Mwaka	M-WAH-kah	Born during the beginning of the year	Swahili	East Africa
Mwalimu	MWAH-lee-moo	Teacher	Swahili	East Africa
Mwanga	MWAH-ngah	Light	Swahili	East Africa
Mwanza	MWAH-n-zah	A Tanzanian town	Swahili	East Africa
Mwapacha	MWAH-pah-chah	Twin	Swahili	East Africa
Mwinyi	M-WEEN-yee	King	Swahili	East Africa
Mwinyimadi	MWEEN-yee-mah-dee	Just ruler	Swahili	East Africa
Mwita	M-WEE-tah	The summoner	Swahili	East Africa
Mzale	M-ZAH-leh	Native	Swahili	East Africa
Mzee	M-ZEH	Elderly and wise, a sage	Swahili	East Africa
Naadir	NAH-deer	Rare	Swahili	East Africa
Naasir	NAH-sir	Defender	Swahili	East Africa
Nabhani	NAHB-hani	Sensible, judicious	Swahili	East Africa
Nabil	NAH-bill	Noble	Swahili	East Africa
Nadhim	NAH-deem	Organizer	Swahili	East Africa
Najub	NAH-joob	Noble	Swahili	East Africa
Nanji	NAHN-jee	Safe	Swahili	East Africa
Nasiir	NAH-sir	Helper	Swahili	East Africa
Nasila	Nah-see-LAH	Honey	Swahili	East Africa
Nasor	NAH-soh	Saved	Swahili	East Africa
Nassor	NAH-sohr	Victorious	Swahili	East Africa
Nathari	NAH-thah-ree	Prose embroidery	Swahili	East Africa
Nemsi	NEHM-see	Respectable	Swahili	East Africa
Nguvumali	GOO-voo-mah-lee	Power is wealth	Swahili	East Africa
Niamoja	Nee-ah-moh-JAH	One purpose	Swahili	East Africa
Nuru	NOO-roo	Born in daylight	Swahili	East Africa

KENYA-TANZANIA

Name	Pronunciation	Meaning	Origin	Region
Nyuni	NYU-nee	Bird	Swahili	East Africa
Oman	OH-man	Influential	Swahili	East Africa
Omari	Oh-MAH-ree	The highest of Muhammads followers	Swahili	East Africa
Omari	Oh-MAH-ree	The highest	Swahili	East Africa
Pandu	PAHN-doo	Artistic	Swahili	East Africa
Pili	PEE-lee	The second born	Swahili	East Africa
Pongwa	Pohn-gwah	Cured	Swahili	East Africa
Popo	POH-poh	Bat, sleeps in the daytime	Swahili	East Africa
Rafiki	RAH-fee-kee	A friend	Swahili	East Africa
Raha	RAH-hah	Joy	Swahili	East Africa
Rahim	RAH-heem	Merciful	Swahili	East Africa
Rajabu	Rah-JAH-boo	Born in the seventh month	Swahili	East Africa
Ramadhani	Rah-mah-DHAH-nee	Born during the month of Ramadan	Swahili	East Africa
Rashaad	Rah-SHAD	Righteous	Swahili	East Africa
Rashad	Rah-SHAD	Righteous	Swahili	East Africa
Rashid	Rah-SHEED	Pious one	Swahili	East Africa
Rashidi	Rah-SHEE-dee	Of good council	Swahili	East Africa
Rasul	RAH-sool	Messenger	Swahili	East Africa
Rauf	Rah-OOF	Kind, merciful	Swahili	East Africa
Rehani	REH-hah-nee	Sweet smell	Swahili	East Africa
Rejalla	REH-jah-lah	God wills it	Swahili	East Africa
Ridha	REE-dah	Contented	Swahili	East Africa
Ridhwani	REED-wah-nee	Permission, agreement	Swahili	East Africa
Rifaa	REE-far	Exalted	Swahili	East Africa
Rijaal	REE-jahl	Man	Swahili	East Africa
Rubama	Roo-BAH-mah	Possibility	Swahili	East Africa

KENYA-TANZANIA

Name	Pronunciation	Meaning	Origin	Region
Rubanza	Roo-BAHN-zah	Courageous	Swahili	East Africa
Rumaliza	Roo-MAH-lee-zah	Deliverance	Swahili	East Africa
Saad	SAH-ahd	Good fortune	Swahili	East Africa
Saalim	SAH-leem	Safe	Swahili	East Africa
Saami	Sah-MEE	Exalted	Swahili	East Africa
Saburi	Sah-BOO-ree	Patience	Swahili	East Africa
Sadiki	Sah-DEE-kee	Faithful	Swahili	East Africa
Saeed	Sah-EED	Happy, fortunate	Swahili	East Africa
Safari	SAH-fah-ree	Journey	Swahili	East Africa
Safwani	SAHF-wah-nee	Sincere	Swahili	East Africa
Saghiri	SAH-gee-ree	Young	Swahili	East Africa
Sahalani	SAH-ha-lah-nee	Ease	Swahili	East Africa
Said	SAY-eed	Happy	Swahili	East Africa
Salaam	SAH-laam	Peace	Swahili	East Africa
Salah	Sah-LAH	Goodness	Swahili	East Africa
Saleh	Sah-LEH	Good	Swahili	East Africa
Salehe	Sah-LEH-he	Good	Swahili	East Africa
Salim	Sah-LEEM	Peace	Swahili	East Africa
Salmini	Sahl-MEE-nee	Saved	Swahili	East Africa
Samir	SAH-meer	Companion	Swahili	East Africa
Sarahani	SAH-rah-hah-nee	Free	Swahili	East Africa
Sarhaan	SAH-haan	Free	Swahili	East Africa
Sefu	SEH-foo	Sword	Swahili	East Africa
Seif	SAY-if	Sword, brave	Swahili	East Africa
Selemani	SEH-leh-mah-nee	Wise, Solomon	Swahili	East Africa
Shaabani	SHAH-bah-nee	Eigth month	Swahili	East Africa
Shaaboni	Shah-BOH-nee	Born in the eigth month	Swahili	East Africa
Shahaab	SHAH-haab	Shooting star	Swahili	East Africa
Shahidi	SHAH-hee-dee	Witness	Swahili	East Africa
Shakwe	SHAH-kweh	A kind of bird	Swahili	East Africa

KENYA-TANZANIA

Name	Pronunciation	Meaning	Origin	Region
Shamakani	SHAH-mah-kah-nee	Presides, leader of the place	Swahili	East Africa
Shambe	SHAHM-beh	Leader	Swahili	East Africa
Sharif	SHAH-reef	Noble	Swahili	East Africa
Shazidi	SHAH-zee-dee	Growth	Swahili	East Africa
Sheikh	SHAY-kih	Leader, elder	Swahili	East Africa
Shibe	Shee-BEH	Satisfaction	Swahili	East Africa
Shibisha	Shee-bee-shah	Satisfy or make satisfied	Swahili	East Africa
Shinda	SHEEN-dah	Conquer, win	Swahili	East Africa
Shinuni	Shee-NUH-nee	Attack	Swahili	East Africa
Shomari	Shoh-MAH-ree	Forceful	Swahili	East Africa
Shujaa	SHOO-jah	Brave	Swahili	East Africa
Shukrani	SHOOK-rah-nee	Grateful	Swahili	East Africa
Sifa	See-FAH	Fame, reputation	Swahili	East Africa
Simai	See-MAH-ee	High	Swahili	East Africa
Simba	SEEM-bah	Lion	Swahili	East Africa
Sinaan	See-NAHN	Spearhead, brave	Swahili	East Africa
Siwatu	See- WAH-too	Born during a time of conflict	Swahili	East Africa
Siwazuri	See-wah-ZOO-ree	They are not nice people	Swahili	East Africa
Songoro	SOHN-goh-roh	Metalsmith	Swahili	East Africa
Stima	STEE-mah	Engine, electric power	Swahili	East Africa
Sudi	Soo-DEE	Good fortune	Swahili	East Africa
Suhuba	Soo-HOO-bah	Friend	Swahili	East Africa
Sultaan	Sool-TAHN	Ruler	Swahili	East Africa
Sultan	Sool-TAHN	Ruler	Swahili	East Africa
Sulubu	SOO-loo-boo	Tough	Swahili	East Africa
Suluhu	Soo-loo-HOO	Peacemaker	Swahili	East Africa
Sumai	Suh-MAH-ee	High	Swahili	East Africa

KENYA-TANZANIA

Name	Pronunciation	Meaning	Origin	Region
Sumait	SUH-mah-it	Reputable	Swahili	East Africa
Suwedi	Su-WEH-dee	Young master	Swahili	East Africa
Suwesi	SUH-weh-see	Rule	Swahili	East Africa
Taalib	TAH-leeb	Seeker of	Swahili	East Africa
Tafiti	TAH-fee-tee	Knowledge seeker	Swahili	East Africa
Taha	TAH-hah	Skillful	Swahili	East Africa
Tajamali	TAH-jah-mah-lee	Favor	Swahili	East Africa
Taji	TAH-jee	Crown	Swahili	East Africa
Tajiri	TAH-jee-ree	Rich, wealthy	Swahili	East Africa
Takata	TAH-kah-tah	Pure, clean	Swahili	East Africa
Takatifu	Tah-kah-tee-FOO	Sacred	Swahili	East Africa
Taki	TAH-kee	God-fearing	Swahili	East Africa
Tarishi	TAH-ree-shee	Messenger	Swahili	East Africa
Tawfiki	TAHW-feek-ee	Divine guidance	Swahili	East Africa
Tayari	TAH-yah-ree	Always prepared	Swahili	East Africa
Tendaji	TEHN-dah-jee	Makes things happen, doer	Swahili	East Africa
Teremesha	TEH-reh-m-shah	Always willing to serve others	Swahili	East Africa
Thaabiti	THAH-bee-tee	Firm, steadfast	Swahili	East Africa
Thairu	THAH-ee-roo	Rebellious	Swahili	East Africa
Thani	TAH-nee	Second one	Swahili	East Africa
Thuweni	THOO-weh-nee	Diminutive of Thani	Swahili	East Africa
Tiifu	Tee-FOO	Loyal, faithful	Swahili	East Africa
Tindo	Teen-DOH	Active	Swahili	East Africa
Tukufu	TUH-koo-fuu	Exalted	Swahili	East Africa
Tulivu	TUH-lee-vuh	Peace and tranquility	Swahili	East Africa
Tumaini	Too-MAH-ee-nee	Hope	Swahili	East Africa
Tumbo	TUHM-boh	Stomach	Swahili	East Africa
Ubaya	OO-bah-yah	Bad feeling	Swahili	East Africa

KENYA-TANZANIA

Name	Pronunciation	Meaning	Origin	Region
Ubora	OO-boh-rah	Excellence	Swahili	East Africa
Ubwa	OOB-wah	Delicate, young	Swahili	East Africa
Ufanisi	OO-fah-nee-see	Prosperity	Swahili	East Africa
Uhuru	OO-hoo-roo	Freedom, liberation	Swahili	East Africa
Uki	Oo-KEE	Sadness	Swahili	East Africa
Ukurugenzi	OO-koo-roo-ghen-zee	Stewardship or leadership	Swahili	East Africa
Uledi	OO-leh-dee	Young man	Swahili	East Africa
Umar	OO-mah	Longevity	Swahili	East Africa
Urafiki	OO-rah-fee-kee	Friendship	Swahili	East Africa
Usaama	OO-sah-mah	Precious	Swahili	East Africa
Ushindi	OO-sheen-dee	Victory	Swahili	East Africa
Vuai	Voo-AH-ee	Fisherman	Swahili	East Africa
Wakili	WAH-kee-lee	Lawyer, representative	Swahili	East Africa
Waziri	WAH-zee-ree	Government minister, advisor	Swahili	East Africa
Yahya	YAH-yah	God's gift	Swahili	East Africa
Yakubu	YAH-koo-buh	Jacob	Swahili	East Africa
Yasini	YAH-see-nee	Rule, principle	Swahili	East Africa
Yusuf	Yoo-SOOF	He shall add to his powers	Swahili	East Africa
Zahir	ZAH-hir	Shining	Swahili	East Africa
Zahor	ZAH-hor	Blooming	Swahili	East Africa
Zahran	ZAH-ran	Shine	Swahili	East Africa
Zahur	Zah-HOOR	Flower	Swahili	East Africa
Zaki	ZAH-kee	Virtuous	Swahili	East Africa
Zakwani	ZAH-kwah-nee	Thriving	Swahili	East Africa
Zalika	ZAH-lee-kah	Born of good family	Swahili	East Africa
Zamoyoni	ZAH-moh-yoh-nee	Of the heart	Swahili	East Africa
Zende	ZEHN-deh	Strong, firm	Swahili	East Africa

KENYA-TANZANIA

Name	Pronunciation	Meaning	Origin	Region
Zuber	ZUH-bah	Brave	Swahili	East Africa
Zuberi	Zoo-BEH-ree	Strong	Swahili	East Africa
Zuher	ZUH-ha	Shining	Swahili	East Africa
Zuhri	ZUH-ree	Good looking	Swahili	East Africa
Zuri	ZUH-ree	Good looking	Swahili	East Africa

MALAWI

Name	Pronunciation	Meaning	Origin	Region
Azibo	A-ZEE-boh	The whole earth	Ngoni	South Africa
Bomani	BOH-MAH-nee	A warrior	Ngoni	South Africa
Bwerani	Bweh-RAH-nee	You are welcome	Ngoni	South Africa
Chabwera	Chah-BWEH-rah	He has arrived at last	Ngoni	South Africa
Chafulumisa	Chah-foo-loo-MEE-sah	Swift	Ngoni	South Africa
Chatha	CHAT-hah	Finality, completion	Ngoni	South Africa
Chatuluka	Chah-too-LOO-kah	A departure	Ngoni	South Africa
Chekandino	Cheh-kan-DEE-noh	Hot and spicy	Yao	South Africa
Chibale	Chee-BAH-leh	Kinship	Ngoni	South Africa
Chifundo	Chee-foo-ndo	Mercy	Chichewa	South Africa
Chigani	Chee-GAH-nee	Hound	Ngoni	South Africa
Chikondi	Chee-ko-ndi	Love	Chichewa	South Africa
Chikosi	Chee-KOH-see	Neck	Ngoni	South Africa
Chikumbu	Chee-KOOM-boo	Knife handle	Yao	South Africa
Chimanga	Chee-MAHN-gah	Maize	Ngoni	South Africa

MALAWI

Name	Pronunciation	Meaning	Origin	Region
Chimsima	Cheem-SEE-mah	Hard porridge	Ngoni	South Africa
Chinangwa	Chee-NANG-gwah	Cassava	Ngoni	South Africa
Chipita	Chee-PEE-TAH	It has gone	Ngoni	South Africa
Chisisi	Chee-SEE-see	A secret	Yao	South Africa
Chisulo	Chee-SOO-loh	Strong as steel	Yao	South Africa
Chitsime	Cheet-SEE-meh	A well	Lomwe	South Africa
Chiwanda	Chee-WAN-dah	Mad	Yao	South Africa
Chiwocha	Chee-WOH-chah	Rooster	Lomwe	South Africa
Chumachienda	Choo-mah-chee-EN-dah	A dignitary is on his way	Lomwe	South Africa
Citiwala	Chee-TWAH-lah	Insect	Yao	South Africa
Citseko	Cheet-SEH-koh	A door	Ngoni	South Africa
Dulani	Doo-LAH-nee	Cutting	Ngoni	South Africa
Fulumirani	Foo-loo-mee-RAH-nee	A journey	Ngoni	South Africa
Funsani	Foon-SAH-nee	A request	Ngoni	South Africa
Gogo	GOH-goh	Like grandfather	Ngoni	South Africa
Kafele	Kah-FEH-leh	Worth dying for	Ngoni	South Africa
Kainwendo	Kahm-WEHN-doh	Leg	Ngoni	South Africa
Kajombo	Kah-JOM-boh	Boot	Yao	South Africa
Kamangeni	Kah-man-CEH-nee	Seems to be related	Ngoni	South Africa
Kambuji	Kahm-BOO-jee	Goat	Ngoni	South Africa
Kamowa	Kah-MOH-wah	Beer	Ngoni	South Africa
Kampibe	Kahm-PEE-beh	Go and look	Ngoni	South Africa
Kamuliva	KAH-moo-lee-vah	Lamentable	Ngoni	South Africa
Kamuzu	KAH-moo-zoo	Medicinal	Ngoni	South Africa
Kanjuchi	Kahn-JOO-chee	A bee	Ngoni	South Africa
Kapeni	Kah-PEH-nee	A sharp blade	Yao	South Africa
Kaphiri	Kah-PEE-ree	A hill	Ngoni	South Africa

MALAWI

Name	Pronunciation	Meaning	Origin	Region
Kasiya	Kah-SEE-yah	A departure	Ngoni	South Africa
Kawduka	Kaw-DOO-kah	Crib	Ngoni	South Africa
Kazemde	Kah-ZEHM-deh	Ambassador	Yao	South Africa
Kondwani	Kon-DWAH-nee	Joyful	Ngoni	South Africa
Kubweza	Koo-BWEH-zah	Give it back	Ngoni	South Africa
Kudyauku	Kooyah-oo-koo	A feast	Ngoni	South Africa
Kumanda	Koo-MAHN-dah	Graveyard	Ngoni	South Africa
Kuthakwakulu	Koo-tah-kwah-KOO-loo	The end of man	Yao	South Africa
Kwacha	KWAH-chah	Morning	Ngoni	South Africa
Kwada	KWAH-dah	Night has fallen	Ngoni	South Africa
Kwayera	Kwah-YEH-rah	Dawn	Ngoni	South Africa
Kwende	KWEHN-deh	Let's go	Ngoni	South Africa
Lamburira	Lam-boo-REE-rah	Clean bush	Ngoni	South Africa
Ligongo	Lee-GOHN-goh	Who is this?	Yao	South Africa
Lin	LEE-oo	Voice	Ngoni	South Africa
Linje	LEEN-jeh	Try it	Yao	South Africa
Lisimba	Lee-SEEM-bah	Lion	Yao	South Africa
Liu	LEE-oo	A voice	Ngoni	South Africa
Lugono	Loo-GOH-noh	Sleep	Ngoni	South Africa
Lukongolo	Loo-KOHN-goh-loh	Leg	Yao	South Africa
Madzimoyo	Mad-zee-MOH-yoh	Water of life	Ngoni	South Africa
Makwangwala	Mah-kwan-GWAH-lah	Crown	Ngoni	South Africa
Malawa	Mah-LAH-wah	Flowers	Yao	South Africa
Mandala	Mahn-DAH-lah	Spectacles	Ngoni	South Africa
Mandondo	Mahn-DOHN-doh	Drops	Ngoni	South Africa
Mapemba	Mah-PEHM-bah	Millet	Ngoni	South Africa
Mapira	Ma-PEE-rah	Millet	Yao	South Africa
Masamba	Mah-SAHM-bah	Leaves	Yao	South Africa

MALAWI

Name	Pronunciation	Meaning	Origin	Region
Masibuwa	Mah-see-BOO-wah	Modern days	Yao	South Africa
Mbiya	M-BEE-yah	Money	Yao	South Africa
Mbizi	M-BEE-zee	To drop in water	Lomwe	South Africa
Mbwelera	M-b weh-LEH-rah	Return	Ngoni	South Africa
Milengalenga	Me-leng-gah-LENG-gah	Heaven	Ngoni	South Africa
Moyenda	Moh -YEHN-dah	On a journey	Ngoni	South Africa
Moyo	MOH-yoh	Life, well being, good health	Ngoni	South Africa
Mpasa	M-PAH-sah	Mat	Ngoni	South Africa
Mpesi	M-PEH-see	Stock of maize	Ngoni	South Africa
Mtima	M-TEE-mah	Heart	Ngoni	South Africa
Mtundu	M-TOON-doo	People, commutlity	Ngoni	South Africa
Mvula	M-VOO-lah	Rain	Ngoni	South Africa
Mwai	M-WAH-ee	Good fortune	Ngoni	South Africa
Ndale	N-DAH-leh	Prankster	Ngoni	South Africa
Ndembo	N-DEHM-boh	Elephant	Yao	South Africa
Ngolinga	N-goh-LEENG-gah	Cry baby	Yao	South Africa
Ngombe	N-GOHM-beh	Cow	Yao	South Africa
Ngunda	N-GOON- dah	Dove	Yao	South Africa
Njete	N-JEH-teh	Salt	Yao	South Africa
Nkuku	N-koo-koo	Rooster	Yao	South Africa
Nsomba	N-SOHM-bah	Fish	Yao	South Africa
Nyemba	N-YEM-bah	Beans	Ngoni	South Africa
Onani	Oh-NAH-nee	Look	Ngoni	South Africa
Roozani	Roh-ZAH-nee	Trick	Ngoni	South Africa
Sabola	Sah-BOH-lah	A hot chili pepper	Ngoni	South Africa
Sekani	Seh-KAH-nee	Laughter	Ngoni	South Africa
Siyani	See- YAH-nee	Relinquish	Ngoni	South Africa

MALAWI

Name	Pronunciation	Meaning	Origin	Region
Thako	TAH-koh	Hip	Ngoni	South Africa
Thambo	TAHM-boh	Ground	Ngoni	South Africa
Thenga	Tehnggah	Bring him	Yao	South Africa
Tiyamike	Tee-ya-mee-keh	Let us give thanks	Chichewa	South Africa
Tsalani	Tsah-LAH-nee	Goodbye	Ngoni	South Africa
Tsekani	Tseh-KAH-nee	Close	Ngoni	South Africa
Tsoka	TSOH-ka	Unlucky	Ngoni	South Africa
Ufa	Oo-fah	Flour	Ngoni	South Africa
Umi	Oo-MEE	Life	Yao	South Africa
Unika	Oo-NEE-kah	Light up	Lomwe	South Africa
Useni	Oo-SEH-nee	Tell me	Yao	South Africa
Usi	OO-see	Smoke	Yao	South Africa
Usiku	Oo-SEE-koo	Night	Ngoni	South Africa
Utni	OO-mee	Life	Yao	South Africa
Zikomo	Zee-KOH-moh	Thank you	Ngoni	South Africa

NIGERIA

Name	Pronunciation	Meaning	Origin	Region
Abayomi	Ah-BAH-yoh-mee	Born to bring me joy	Yoruba	West Africa
Abegunde	Ah-beh-GOON-deh	Born during holiday	Yoruba	West Africa
Abejide	Ah-beh-JEE-deh	Born during winter	Yoruba	West Africa
Abiade	AH-bee-ah-DEH	Born of royal parents	Yoruba	West Africa
Abidogun	Ah-BEE-doo-goon	Born before the war	Yoruba	West Africa
Abimbola	Ah-BEEM-boh-lah	Born rich	Yoruba	West Africa

NIGERIA

Name	Pronunciation	Meaning	Origin	Region
Abiodun	Ah-BEE-oh-doon	Born at the time of a festival	Yoruba	West Africa
Abiola	Ah-BEE-oh-lah	Born in honor	Yoruba	West Africa
Abiona	Ah-BEE-oh-nah	Born during a journey	Yoruba	West Africa
Abioye	Ah-BEE-oh-yeh	Born during coronation	Yoruba	West Africa
Ade	Ah-DEH	Royal one	Yoruba	West Africa
Adeagbo	Ah-DEH-ag-boh	He brings royal honor	Yoruba	West Africa
Adebamgbe	Ah-DEH-bam-beh	Royalty dwells with me	Yoruba	West Africa
Adebayo	Ah-DEH-bah-yoh	He came in a joyful time	Yoruba	West Africa
Adeboro	Ah-DEH-boh-roh	Royalty comes into wealth	Yoruba	West Africa
Adedapo	Ah-DEH-dah-poh	Royalty brings the people together	Yoruba	West Africa
Adegoke	Ah-DEH-goh-keh	The crown has been exalted	Yoruba	West Africa
Adejola	Ah-DEH-joh-lah	The crown feeds on honors	Yoruba	West Africa
Adelabu	Ah-DEH-lah-boo	The crown passed through deep water	Yoruba	West Africa
Adelaja	Ah-DEH-lah-jah	The crown settles a quarrel	Yoruba	West Africa
Ademola	Ah-DEH-moh-lah	A crown is added to my wealth	Yoruba	West Africa
Adenrele	Ah-dey-ren-lay	The crown has headed home to roost	Yoruba	West Africa
Adesola	Ah-DEH-soh-lah	The crown honored us	Yoruba	West Africa
Adetokunbo	Ah-DEH-toh-koon-boh	Honor came from over the seas	Yoruba	West Africa

NIGERIA

Name	Pronunciation	Meaning	Origin	Region
Adewole	Ah-DEH-woh-leh	Royalty enters the house	Yoruba	West Africa
Adeyemi	Ah-deh-yeh-MEE	The crown suits me well	Yoruba	West Africa
Adeyemi	Har dey yeh mi	Crown fits me	Yoruba	West Africa
Adigun	Ah-dee-GOON	Righteous	Yoruba	West Africa
Adisa	Ah-dee-SAH	One who makes his meaning clear	Yoruba	West Africa
Adjo	Ah-dee-OH	Be righteous	Yoruba	West Africa
Adubi	Ah-doo-BEE	Born to be pleasant	Yoruba	West Africa
Afiba	Ah-FEE-bah	By the sea	Yoruba	West Africa
Aiyetoro	Ah- YEH-toh-roh	Peace on earth	Yoruba	West Africa
Ajagbe	Ah-jahg-BEH	He carries off the prize	Yoruba	West Africa
Ajamu	Ah-jah-MOO	He fights for what he wants	Yoruba	West Africa
Ajani	Ah-jah-NEE	He fights for possession	Yoruba	West Africa
Ajayi	Ah-JAH-yee	Born face-down	Yoruba	West Africa
Akanni	Ah-KAHN-nee	Our encounter brings possessions	Yoruba	West Africa
Akinkawon	Ah-keen-KAH-wohn	Bravery pacified them	Yoruba	West Africa
Akinlabi	Ah-KEEN-lah-bee	We have a boy	Yoruba	West Africa
Akinlana	Ah-keen-LAH-nah	Valor	Yoruba	West Africa
Akin	Ah-KEENS	Brave boy	Yoruba	West Africa
Akinsanya	Ah-KEEN-sahn-yah	The hero avenges	Yoruba	West Africa
Akinsegun	Ah-keen-sheh-GOON	Valor conquers	Yoruba	West Africa
Akinseye	Ah-KEEN-sheh-yeh	Valor acts honorably	Yoruba	West Africa
Akinsiju	Ah-KEEN-shee-joo	Valor awakes	Yoruba	West Africa

NIGERIA

Name	Pronunciation	Meaning	Origin	Region
Akintunde	Ah-KEEN-toon-deh	A boy has come again	Yoruba	West Africa
Akinwole	Ah-KEEN-woh-leh	Valor enters the house	Yoruba	West Africa
Akinwunmi	Ah-KEEN-woon-mee	Valor is pleasing to me	Yoruba	West Africa
Akinyele	Ah-keen-YEH-leh	Valor benefits this house	Yoruba	West Africa
Akoni	Ah-KOH-nee	It is my turn	Yoruba	West Africa
Alonge	Ah-LOHN-geh	A tall and skinny boy	Yoruba	West Africa
Amadi	Ah-MAH-dee	Seemed destined to die at birth	Benin	West Africa
Animashaun	AH-nee-mah-shohn	Generous	Yoruba	West Africa
Aondohimba	Ah-ohn-doh-HEEM-bah	God is above all things on earth	Tiv	West Africa
Apara	Ah-PAH-rah	Child that comes and goes	Yoruba	West Africa
Ayinde	Ah-yeen-DEH	We gave praises and he came	Yoruba	West Africa
Ayo	AH-yo	Happiness	Yoruba	West Africa
Ayodele	Ah-YOH-deh-leh	Joy enters the house	Yoruba	West Africa
Azagba	Ah-ZAH-bah	Born out of town	Benin	West Africa
Azikiwe	Ah-ZEE-kee-weh	Full of vigor	Ibo	West Africa
Babafemi	Bah-BAH-feh-mee	Father loves me	Yoruba	West Africa
Babatunde	Bah-bah-TOON-deh	Father returns	Yoruba	West Africa
Babatunji	Bah-bah-TOON-jee	Father returns again	Yoruba	West Africa
Balogun	Bah-LOH-GOON	A general	Yoruba	West Africa
Bandele	Ban-DEH-leh	Born away from home	Yoruba	West Africa

NIGERIA

Name	Pronunciation	Meaning	Origin	Region
Banjoko	BAN-joh-koh	Stay with me and wander no more	Yoruba	West Africa
Bankole	BAN-koh-leh	Help build our house	Yoruba	West Africa
Bem	Behm	Peace	Tiv	West Africa
Boseda	BOH-seh-dah	Born on Sunday	Tiv	West Africa
Chijioke	CHEE-jee-oh-keh	God gives talent	Ibo	West Africa
Chike	CHEE-keh	The power of God	Ibo	West Africa
Chinelo	CHEE-neh-loh	Thoughts of God	Ibo	West Africa
Chinua	CHEE-noo-ah	Leave the battle for God	Ibo	West Africa
Chioh	CHEE-oh	Power of God	Ibo	West Africa
Chioke	CHEE-oh-keh	Gift of God	Ibo	West Africa
Chukwudiogo	Chukwu-de-ogo	God is blessing	Ibo	West Africa
Chukwueneka	Choo-koo-eh-NEH-kah	God has dealt kindly with us	Ibo	West Africa
Dada	DAH-dah	Child with curly hair	Yoruba	West Africa
Danjuma	Dan-joo-MAH	Born on Friday	Hausa	West Africa
Danladi	Dan-LAH-dee	Born on Sunday	Hausa	West Africa
Dibia	DEE-bee-ah	Healer	Ibo	West Africa
Diji	DEE-jee	A farmer	Ibo	West Africa
Dunsimi	Doon-SEE-mee	Don't die before me	Yoruba	West Africa
Durojaiye	Doo-roh-jah-yeh	Slow down and enjoy the world	Yoruba	West Africa
Eberegbulam	Eh-BEH-reh-boo-lam	My kindness shall not destroy me	Ibo	West Africa
Ehidiamen	Eh-EE-Dee-Amen	God is with Me	Edo	West Africa
Ehioze	Eh-EE-oh-ZAY	Above the envy of others	Benin	West Africa
Ekundayo	Eh-KOON-dah-yoh	Sorrow becomes happiness	Yoruba	West Africa

87

NIGERIA

Name	Pronunciation	Meaning	Origin	Region
Enobakhare	Eh-noh-bah-KAH-reh	The King's word	Benin	West Africa
Esosa	E so sa	God's blessing	Edo	West Africa
Etinosa	Ety-no-sah	God's power	Edo	West Africa
Ewansiha	Eh-wan-see-HAH	Secrets are not for sale	Benin	West Africa
Eze	Eh-ZEH	King	Ibo	West Africa
Ezeamaka	EH-zeh-ah-mah-kah	As splendid as the king	Ibo	West Africa
Ezenachi	Eh-zeh-nah-chee	The king rules	Ibo	West Africa
Ezeoha	EH-zeh-oh-hah	A people's king	Ibo	West Africa
Foluke	Foh-LOO-keh	Placed in God's hands	Yoruba	West Africa
Gowon	GOH-wohn	Rainmaker	Tiv	West Africa
Ibrahim	EE-brah-heem	My father is exalted	Hausa	West Africa
Idogbe	Ee-doh-BEH	Second born after twins	Yoruba	West Africa
Idowu	Ee-DOH-woo	Born after twins	Yoruba	West Africa
Ikechi	E kay chi	God's power	Igbo	West Africa
Imarogbe	Ee-MAH-roh-beh	Child born to a good family	Benin	West Africa
Iroagbulam	Ee-ROH-eh-boo-lam	Let not enmity destroy me	Ibo	West Africa
Iyapo	Ee-YAH-po	Many trials	Yoruba	West Africa
Jaja	JAH-jah	Honored one	Ibo	West Africa
Jibade	Jee-bah-DEH	Royalty	Yoruba	West Africa
Jumoke	Joo-MOH-keh	Everyone loves the child	Yoruba	West Africa
Kayode	KAH-yoh-deh	One who brought joy	Yoruba	West Africa
Kehinde	Keh-HEEN-deh	Second born of twins	Yoruba	West Africa

NIGERIA

Name	Pronunciation	Meaning	Origin	Region
Kosoko	Koh-SOH-koh	No hoe to dig a grave	Yoruba	West Africa
Kumapayi	Kuh-Ma-per-Yi	Death preserve this life	Yoruba	West Africa
Kunle	KOON-leh	Our home is filled with honors	Yoruba	West Africa
Iyapo	Ee-YAH-po	Many trials	Yoruba	West Africa
Madu	MAH-doo	People	Ibo	West Africa
Mazi	MAH-zee	Sir	Ibo	West Africa
Modupe	Moh-DOO-peh	Thank you	Yoruba	West Africa
Mongo	MOHN-goh	Famous	Yoruba	West Africa
Namdi	Nahm-DEE	Father's name lives on	Ibo	West Africa
Ngozi	N-GOH-zee	Blessing	Ibo	West Africa
Nmeregini	N-MEH-reh-ghee-nee	What have I done?	Ibo	West Africa
Nnamdi	N-NAHM-dee	Fathers name lives on	Ibo	West Africa
Nnanna	N-NAHN-nah	Grandfather	Ibo	West Africa
Nosakhere	Noh-SAH-keh-reh	Gods way is the only way	Benin	West Africa
Nwabudike	NWAH-boo-dee-KEH	Son is the fathers power	Ibo	West Africa
Oba	AW-bah	King	Yoruba	West Africa
Obadele	Aw-bah-DEH-leh	The king arrives at the house	Yoruba	West Africa
Obafemi	Aw-bah-FEH-mee	The king likes me	Yoruba	West Africa
Obanjoko	Aw-ban-JOH-koh	The king is enthroned	Yoruba	West Africa
Obaseki	Aw-BAH-seh-kee	The king's influence goes beyond the market	Benin	West Africa
Obataiye	Aw-bah-TAH-ee-yeh	King of the world	Yoruba	West Africa

NIGERIA

Name	Pronunciation	Meaning	Origin	Region
Obawole	Aw-bah-WOH-leh	The king enters the house	Yoruba	West Africa
Obayana	Aw-bah-YAH-nah	The king warms himself at the fire	Yoruba	West Africa
Ode	Oh-DEH	One born along the road	Benin	West Africa
Odiinkemelu	Oh-deem-KEH-meh-loo	I have done nothing wrong	Ibo	West Africa
Odion	OH-dee-on	First of twins	Benin	West Africa
Ogbonna	Oh-BOHN-nah	Image of his father	Ibo	West Africa
Ogonna	Oh-GOH-nah	Father in law	Ibo	West Africa
Ogunkeye	Oh-GOON-keh-yeh	The god Ogun has gathered honor	Yoruba	West Africa
Ogunsanwo	Oh-GOON-shahn-wo	Help comes from Ogun, god of war	Yoruba	West Africa
Ogunsheye	Oh-GOON-sheh-yeh	The god Ogun had acted honorably	Yoruba	West Africa
Ojo	Oh-JOH	Born in a difficult delivery	Yoruba	West Africa
Okafor	Oh-KAH-for	Born on Afor market day	Ibo	West Africa
Okanlawon	Oh-kahn-LAH-wohn	Son born after several daughters	Yoruba	West Africa
Okechuku	Oh-keh-CHOO-koo	Gods gift	Ibo	West Africa
Okeke	Oh-KEH-keh	Born on the market day	Ibo	West Africa
Okonkwo	Oh-kohnq-kwoh	Born on Nkwo market day	Ibo	West Africa
Okorie	Oh-KOH-ree-eh	Born on Oryo market day	Ibo	West Africa
Okpara	Ok-PAH-rah	First son	Ibo	West Africa
Ola	AW-lah	Wealth	Yoruba	West Africa
Oladele	Aw-lah-DEH-leh	Honors, wealth arrive at home	Yoruba	West Africa

NIGERIA

Name	Pronunciation	Meaning	Origin	Region
Olafemi	Aw-lah-FEH-mee	Wealth, honor favors me	Yoruba	West Africa
Olamina	Aw-lah-MEE-nah	This is my wealth	Yoruba	West Africa
Olaniyan	Aw-lah-NEE-yahn	Honors surround me	Yoruba	West Africa
Olateju	Or-lah- teh ju	Abundant and renowned wealth	Yoruba	West Africa
Olatunji	Aw-lah-TOON-jee	Honor reawakens	Yoruba	West Africa
Olu	OH-loo	Preeminent	Yoruba	West Africa
Olubayo	Oh-loo-BAH-yoh	Highest joy	Yoruba	West Africa
Olubunmi	Oh-loo-BOON-mee	God blessed me with a gift	Yoruba	West Africa
Olufemi	Oh-loo-FEH-mee	God loves me	Yoruba	West Africa
Olugbala	Oh-LOO-bah-lah	Savior of the people	Yoruba	West Africa
Olugbodi	Oh-LOO-boh-dee	Child born with extra fingers or toes	Yoruba	West Africa
Olujimi	Oh-loo-JEE-mee	God gave me this	Yoruba	West Africa
Olukayode	Oh-loo-KAH-yoh-deh	My lord brings happiness	Yoruba	West Africa
Olumide	Olr-loo-MEE-deh	My lord arrives	Yoruba	West Africa
Olusegun	Oh-loo-shehgoon	God is the victor	Yoruba	West Africa
Olusoga	Oh-Loo –Shaw-gar	God displays her mastery	Yoruba	West Africa
Olusola	Oh-LOO-shoh-lah	God has blessed me	Yoruba	West Africa
Olutosin	Oh-loo-TOH-seen	God deserves to be praised	Yoruba	West Africa
Oluwa	O-LOO-wah	Our lord	Yoruba	West Africa
Oluyemi	Oh-loo-YEH-mee	Fulfillment from God	Yoruba	West Africa
Omolara	Oh-MOHN-lah-rah	Child born at the right time	Benin	West Africa

NIGERIA

Name	Pronunciation	Meaning	Origin	Region
Omorede	Oh-moh-REH-deh	Prince	Benin	West Africa
Omoruyi	Oh-moh-ROO-yee	Respect from God	Benin	West Africa
Omotunde	Oh-,iioh-TOON-deli	A child comes again	Yoruba	West Africa
Omwokha	Ohm-WOH-kah	Second of twins	Benin	West Africa
Onipede	Oh-nee-PEH-dell	The consoler will come	Yoruba	West Africa
Onuwachi	Oh-too-WAH-chee	Gods world	Ibo	West Africa
Onyebuchi	On-yeh-BOO-chee	Who is God	Ibo	West Africa
Onyemachi	On-yeh-MAH-chee	Who knows Gods will	Ibo	West Africa
Orji	OR-jee	Mighty tree	Ibo	West Africa
Osagboro	Oh-SAH-boh-roh	There is only one God	Benin	West Africa
Osahar	Oh-SAH-har	God listens	Benin	West Africa
Osakhare	Osah-khare	God said	Edo	West Africa
Osakwe	Oh-SAH-kweh	God agrees	Benin	West Africa
Osayaba	Oh-sah-YAH-bah	God forgives	Benin	West Africa
Osayande	Oh-sah-YAHN-deh	God owns the world	Benin	West Africa
Osayiniwese	Oh-sah-eern-WEH-seh	God made me whole	Benin	West Africa
Osaze	Oh-SAH-zeh	Loved by God	Benin	West Africa
Oseghae	Ose-gha-e	It's God that giveth	Ishan	West Africa
Ottah	Ot-TAH	Child thin at birth	Urhobo	West Africa
Owoduni	Oh-woh-DOON-nee	It is nice to have money	Yoruba	West Africa
Shangobunmi	Shang-goh-BOON-mee	A child given by the God Shango	Yoruba	West Africa
Sowande	Shoh-WAHN-deh	The wise healer sought me out	Yoruba	West Africa
Taiwo	TAH-ee-woh	First born of twins	Yoruba	West Africa
Teremun	TEH-reh-moon	Fathers acceptance	Tiv	West Africa

NIGERIA

Name	Pronunciation	Meaning	Origin	Region
Tor	Toor	King	Tiv	West Africa
Tyehimba	Tah-ye-heem-BAH	We stand as a nation	Tiv	West Africa
Unuigbe	Who–noo-Hi bay	Mouth does not kill	Edo	West Africa
Uche	Who-CHEH	Thought	Ibo	West Africa
Uyiosa	Who-yi-oh-sah	God's honor	Edo	West Africa
Wafor	WAH-for	Born on Afor market day	Ibo	West Africa
Weke	WEH-keh	Born on Eke market day	Ibo	West Africa
Worie	WOH-ree-eh	Born on Afor market day	Ibo	West Africa
Yohance	Yoh-HAHN-seh	Gods gift	Hausa	West Africa

NORTH AFRICAN ARAB COUNTRIES

Name	Pronunciation	Meaning	Origin	Region
Akil	Ah-KEEL	Intelligent, one who uses reason	Arabic	North Africa
Asim	Ah-SEEM	Protector, defender	Arabic	North Africa
Aswad	Ahss-WAHD	Black	Arabic	North Africa
Khalid	KHAH-leed	Eternal	Arabic	North Africa
Muslim	MOO-slim	Believer	Arabic	North Africa
Naeem	Nah-EEM	Benevolent	Arabic	North Africa
Nizam	Nee-ZAHM	Disciplinarian, arranger	Arabic	North Africa
Omar	OH-mar	The highest of Muhammads followers	Arabic	North Africa
Shakir	SHAH-keer	Thankful	Arabic	North Africa

NORTH AFRICAN ARAB COUNTRIES

Name	Pronunciation	Meaning	Origin	Region
Sulaiman	Soo-lah-ee-MAHN	Peaceful	Arabic	North Africa
Tabari	TAH-bah-ree	Famous Muslim historian	Arabic	North Africa
Tahir	TAH-heer	Clean, pure	Arabic	North Africa
Talib	TAH-lib	Seeker	Arabic	North Africa
Tarik	TAH-rick	Muslim general who conquered Spain	Arabic	North Africa
Aitiya	Iteeyah	God Given	Arabic	North Africa
Jamil	Jameel	Handsome	Arabic	North Africa
Karim	Kareem	Generous	Arabic	North Africa
Thabit	TAH-bit	Firm	Arabic	North Africa
Zaid	ZAH-ee-id	Increase, growth	Arabic	North Africa

RWANDA

Name	Pronunciation	Meaning	Region
Dukuzumuremyi	Doo-koo-zoo-moo-REM-yee	Praise be to God	East Africa
Gahiji	Gah-HEE-jee	The hunter	East Africa
Habimana	Hah-bee-MAH-nah	God exists	East Africa
Hakizimana	Hah-kee-zee-MAH-nah	It is God who saves	East Africa
Nkundiushuti	N-koon-deen-SHOO-tee	I love people	East Africa
Nyillingondo	Nee-yee-leen-GOHN-do	Handsome	East Africa
Runihura	Roo-nee-HOO-rah	One who smashes to bits	East Africa
Sebahive	Seh-bah-HEE-veh	Bringer of good fortune	East Africa
Sentwali	Sehn-TWAH-lee	Courageos	East Africa

SENEGAL

Name	Pronunciation	Meaning	Origin	Region
Diallo	DEE-ah-loh	Bold one	Malinke	West Africa

SOUTH AFRICA

Name	Pronunciation	Meaning	Origin	Region
Ayize	Ah-yee-ZEH	Let it happen	Zulu	South Africa
Chihambuane	Chee-ham-boo-AH-neh	Sweet potatoes	Bachopi	South Africa
Chuguel	CHOO-goo-el	Sugar	Bachopi	South Africa
Dingane	Deen-GAH-neh	One who is searching	Zulu	South Africa
Mpumelele	M-poo-meh-LEH-loh	Success	Zulu	South Africa
Mthuthuzeli	M-too-too-ZEH-lee	Comforter	Xhosa	South Africa
Nkosi	N-KOH-see	Ruler	Zulu	South Africa
Nolizwe	Noh-leez-WEH	The nation	Xhosa	South Africa
Nonceba	Nong-CHEH-bah	Mercy	Xhosa	South Africa
Paki	PAH-kee	A witness	Xhosa	South Africa
Sigidi	See-GHEE-dee	One thousand	Zulu	South Africa
Sipho	See-POH	Gift	Zulu	South Africa
Sipliwo	See-PLEE-woh	Gift	Xhosa	South Africa
Thandiwe	Tahn-DEE-weh	Beloved	Zulu	South Africa
Themba	TEHM-bah	Hope	Xhosa	South Africa
Uuka	Oo-OO-kah	Arise	Xhosa	South Africa

TANZANIA

Name	Pronunciation	Meaning	Origin	Region
Ambakisye	Am-bah-KEES-yeh	God has been merciful to me	Ndali	East Africa
Ambidwile	Am-bee-DWEE-leh	God has convinced me	Nyakyusa	East Africa
Ambilikile	Am-bee-lee-KEE-leh	God called me	Nyakyusa	East Africa
Ambokile	Am-bo-KEE-leh	God has redeemed me	Nyakyusa	East Africa
Ambonisye	Ahm-BOH-nee-say	God has rewarded me	Nyakyusa	East Africa
Andalwisye	Ahn-dal-WEES-yeh	God has shown me the way	Nyakyusa	East Africa
Andengwisye	Ahn-deng-gwees-yeh	God has claimed me	Nyakyusa	East Africa
Andongwisye	An-DONG-wee-say	God has led me	Nyakyusa	East Africa
Andwele	Ahn-DWEH-leh	God brought me	Nyakyusa	East Africa
Angolwisye	Ahn-gohl-wees-yeh	God has guided me	Nyakyusa	East Africa
Angosisye	Ahn-goh-sees-yeh	God sanctified me	Nyakyusa	East Africa
Anyabwile	Ahn-yah-BWEE-leh	God has unchained me	Nyakyusa	East Africa
Anyelwiswe	Ahn-yel-WEES-weh	God has purified me	Nyakyusa	East Africa
Asukile	Ah-soo-KEE-leh	The Lord has washed me	Nyakyusa	East Africa
Ipyana	Eep-YAH-nah	Grace	Nyakyusa	East Africa
Kajakafwile	Kah-jah-kah-FWEE-leh	The town is dead	Nyakyusa	East Africa
Masomakali	Mah-soh-mah-KAH-lee	Sharp eyes	Nyakyusa	East Africa
Masopakyindi	Mah-soh-pack-YEEN-dee	Eyes like hard porridge	Nyakyusa	East Africa
Motogusinile	Moh-toh-goo-see-NEE-leh	The first is out	Nyakyusa	East Africa
Mposi	M-POH-see	Blacksmith	Nyakyusa	East Africa

TANZANIA

Name	Pronunciation	Meaning	Origin	Region
Mwamba	M-WAM-bah	Strong	Nyakyusa	East Africa
Mwanyambi	M-wan-YAM-bee	Bag	Nyakyusa	East Africa
Mwinyimkuu	M-ween-yeem-KOO	Great king	Zaramo	East Africa
Ndweleifwa	N-dweh-leh-EEF-wah	I came with morning	Nyakyusa	East Africa
Ngonepe	N-goh-NEH-poh	Repose	Nyakyusa	East Africa
Nikusubila	Nee-koo-see-BEE-lah	Hopeful	Nyakyusa	East Africa
Tukupasya	Too-koo-PASS-ya	We are afraid	Nyakyusa	East Africa
Tuponile	Toc-poh-NEE-leh	We are saved	Nyakyusa	East Africa
Watende	Wah-TEHN-deh	There shall be no revenge	Nyakyusa	East Africa

UGANDA

Name	Pronunciation	Meaning	Origin	Region
Akiki	Ah-kee-EE-kee	Friend	Ankole	East Africa
Balondemu	Bah-lon-DEH-moo	The chosen one	Musoga	East Africa
Gwandoya	Gwan-DOH-yah	Met with unhappiness	Luganda	East Africa
Kadokechi	Kah-doh-KEH-chee	Bitter soup	Mudama	East Africa
Kigongo	Kee-GONG-goh	Born before twins	Luganda	East Africa
Kizza	Keez-SAH	Born after twins	Luganda	East Africa
Lutalo	LOO-tah-loh	Warrior	Luganda	East Africa
Luzige	Loo-zee-GHEH	Locust	Mugwere	East Africa
Madongo	Mah-DOHN-goh	Uncircumcised	Luganda	East Africa
Magomu	Mah-goh-MOO	Younger of twins	Luganda	East Africa
Mulogo	MOO-loh-goh	A wizard	Musoga	East Africa
Munanire	Moo-nah-nee-REH	Has more than his share	Luganda	East Africa

UGANDA

Name	Pronunciation	Meaning	Origin	Region
Munyiga	Moon-YEE-gah	One who presses others	Mukiga	East Africa
Musoke	Moo-soh-KEH	Cannot be introduced	Buganda	East Africa
Najja	NAH-jah	Born after	Luganda	East Africa
Nakisisa	Nah-kee-SEE-sah	Child of the shadows	Buganda	East Africa
Ogwambi	Oh-GWAHM-bee	Always unfortunate	Luganda	East Africa
Ojore	Oh-joh-REH	A warrior	Ateso	East Africa
Ojore	Oh-joh-REH	A man of war	Ateso	East Africa
Wemusa	Weh-moo-SAH	Never satisfied with his possessions	Luganda	East Africa
Zesiro	Zeh-SEE-roh	Elder of twins	Luganda	East Africa
Zilabamuzale	Zee-lah-bah-moo-ZAH-leh	Sickly child	Luganda	East Africa

ZIMBABWE

Name	Pronunciation	Meaning	Origin	Region
Banga	BAHN-ga	Sword	Shona	South Africa
Chenzira	Chen-SEE-rah	Born on a journey	Shona	South Africa
Chinouyazue	Chee-noo-yah-ZWEH	Will be back again	Shona	South Africa
Chionesu	Choh-NEH-soo	A guiding light	Shona	South Africa
Chuma	CHOO-mah	Wealth	Shona	South Africa
Dakarai	Dah-kah-RAH-ee	Joy	Shona	South Africa
Gamba	GAM-bah	Warrior	Shona	South Africa
Garai	GAH-rah-ee	Calm	Shona	South Africa
Goredenna	Goh-reh-deh-NAH	A storm cloud	Shona	South Africa
Hondo	HOHN-doh	War	Shona	South Africa

ZIMBABWE

Name	Pronunciation	Meaning	Origin	Region
Kokayi	Koh-KAH-yee	He summons the people	Shona	South Africa
Maideyi	Mah-EE-deh-yee	What did you want?	Shona	South Africa
Mashama	Mah-SHAH-mah	You are surprised	Shona	South Africa
Muchaneta	Moo-chah-NEH-tah	You will get tired	Shona	South Africa
Mudada	Moo-DAH-dah	The provider	Shona	South Africa
Mwanyisa	M-WAHN-yee-sah	Accept defeat	Shona	South Africa
Paradzanai	Pah-rah-zah-NAH-ee	Keep it aside	Shona	South Africa
Pepukayi	Peh-poo-KAH-yee	Wake up	Shona	South Africa
Petiri	PEH-tee-ree	Here we are	Shona	South Africa
Peyisai	Peh-yee-SAH-ee	Conclusion	Shona	South Africa
Rudo	ROO-doh	Love	Shona	South Africa
Runako	Roo-NAH-koh	Handsome	Shona	South Africa
Sekayi	Seh-KAH-yee	Laughter	Shona	South Africa
Sundai	Soon-DAH-ee	To push	Shona	South Africa
Tichawonna	Tee-CHAH-oh-nah	We shall see	Shona	South Africa
Zuka	Zoo-KAH	Money	Shona	South Africa

ABOUT THE AUTHOR

Bunmi Adebayo a.k.a "OPJ" or "Opeji", a Nigerian-American is an alumnus of both the University of Ife, (Now OAU) Ile- Ife Nigeria, and University of Missouri- Columbia, Graduate School, in the United states where he graduated in International relations and New Media respectively. He's also taken Project management courses at the Rutgers University- New Brunswick NJ, also in the United States. 'OPJ, as he''s fondly called attended the prestigious Abeokuta Grammar School and Ogun State Polytechnic both in Abeokuta Nigeria, in the mid 70's and early 80's for his High school and "A" levels education respectively.

Bunmi, currently based in New Jersey in the United States was born in his native home town of Abeokuta, Ogun state Nigeria in the mid 60,s to a family of seven in which he is the second child. The author is married to his friend, 'Remi, (nee Macjob) and currently blessed with three children (Temilade, Oyinade, and Omolade).

Bunmi has been working in Information technology as Web Administrator since the late 90,s with a stint at the Journal of Commerce (then, a subsidiary of London Economist) and XO communications, both in the United States.

His challenges in his days at the University of Ife on race and International relations culminated in his study of the history of the Africans in diasporas, especially North, South and Central America and the attendant effect on their country''s international relations with Africa. This publication 'Dictionary of African names" is his contribution to the closure of the divide created by the middle passage and an eventual culturally connected committee of African nations both in the homeland and diasporas.

'Bunmi adores Chief Obafemi Awolowo (Late Nigerian Nationalist), and especially his popular saying 'After darkness comes glorious dawn".

'Bunmi Adebayo can be reached at opeji@hotmail.com.

Printed in the United States
78402LV00004B/384